FLIGHT

ALSO BY LINDA BIERDS

FLIGHT

New and
Selected Poems

———

LINDA BIERDS

A MARIAN WOOD BOOK
Published by G. P. Putnam's Sons
a member of Penguin Group (USA) Inc.
New York

A MARIAN WOOD BOOK
Published by G. P. Putnam's Sons
Publishers Since 1838
a member of the Penguin Group
Penguin Group (USA) Inc., 375 Hudson Street, New York, New York 10014, USA ·
Penguin Group (Canada), 90 Eglinton Avenue East, Suite 700, Toronto,
Ontario M4P 2Y3, Canada (a division of Pearson Canada Inc.) ·
Penguin Books Ltd, 80 Strand, London WC2R 0RL, England ·
Penguin Ireland, 25 St Stephen's Green, Dublin 2, Ireland
(a division of Penguin Books Ltd) · Penguin Group (Australia),
250 Camberwell Road, Camberwell, Victoria 3124, Australia
(a division of Pearson Australia Group Pty Ltd) · Penguin Books India Pvt Ltd,
11 Community Centre, Panchsheel Park, New Delhi–110 017, India ·
Penguin Group (NZ), 67 Apollo Drive, Rosedale, North Shore 0632, New Zealand
(a division of Pearson New Zealand Ltd) · Penguin Books (South Africa) (Pty) Ltd,
24 Sturdee Avenue, Rosebank, Johannesburg 2196, South Africa

Penguin Books Ltd, Registered Offices: 80 Strand, London WC2R 0RL, England

Library of Congress Cataloging-in-Publication Data
Bierds, Linda.
Flight: new and selected poems: Linda Bierds.
p.   cm.
"A Marian Wood book."
ISBN 978-0-399-15525-3
I. Title.
PS3552.I357A6   2008   2008028145
811'.54—dc22

Printed in the United States of America
1 3 5 7 9 10 8 6 4 2

Book design by Jessica Shatan Heslin / Studio Shatan, Inc.

For Marian Wood, all

ACKNOWLEDGMENTS

I am grateful to Ahsahta Press for allowing me to reprint these poems from *Flights of the Harvest-Mare:* "Lesson: The Spider's Eighth Eye," "Mid-Plains Tornado," "Mirror," "Tongue," and "Zuni Potter: Drawing the Heartline."

My thanks as well to The Rockefeller Foundation for a month-long residency in Bellagio, Italy, during which much of this book was shaped, and to the editors of journals in which a number of new poems first appeared:

Alhambra Poetry Calendar (2008): "Navigation"; *The Atlantic Monthly:* "Sketchbook"; *Bellingham Review:* "Exhibition of a Rhinoceros at Venice"; *Blackbird.com:* "Meriwether and the Magpie"; *Field:* "Salvage"; *The Journal:* "Thoughts Toward the First Christmas Lecture"; *The Laurel Review:* "Dürer near Fifty"; *Northwest Review:* "From the Sea of Tranquillity"; *Poetry:* "Accountancy: Dürer in Antwerp" and "Flight"; *Poetry Northwest:* "Fragments from Venice: Albrecht Dürer" and "From Campalto."

Finally, and always, my gratitude to Sydney Kaplan, for the life that led to this work.

CONTENTS

New Poems

■■■ This symbol is used to indicate a space between stanzas whenever such space is lost in pagination.

FROM *Flights of the Harvest-Mare* (1985)

AND *The Stillness, the Dancing* (1988)

———

The Stillness, the Dancing

I am indefinitely capable of wonder.
—FEDERICO FELLINI

Long ago, in the forests of southern Europe,
just south of Mâcon, a woman died in childbirth.
She was taken, by custom, to the small slate
lip of a mountain. Legs bound at the knees
she was left facing west, thick with her still child.

Century by century, nothing disturbed them

so that now
the bones of the woman cup the small bones
of the child: the globe of its head angled
there, in the paddle and stem of her hips.

It is winter, just after midday. Slowly,
shudder by civilized shudder, a train slips over
the mountain, reveals to its weary riders

something white, then again, something
white at the side of the eye. They straighten,
place their lips to the glass, and there, far
below, this delicate, bleached pattern,
like the spokes of a bamboo cage.
What, someone whispers, and What, What,
word after word bouncing back from its blossom
of vapor, the woman and child appearing,
disappearing, as the train slips down through the alders—

...
until they are brands of the eyelid, until they are
stories, until, thick-soled and silent,
each rider squats with a blessing of ocher.

And so there are stories. Mortar. A little stratum
under the toenails. A train descends from a mountain,
levels out, circles a field where a team of actors
mimics a picnic. The billowing children.
On the table, fruit, a great calabash of chilled fish.
And over it all, a beloved uncle, long mad,
sits in the crotch of an oak tree.

He hears to his right, the compressed blare
of a whistle—each sound wave approaching shorter, shorter,
like words on a window, then just as the engine passes,
the long playing out.
He smiles as the blare seeps over
the actors, the pasture, the village

where now, in the haze of a sudden snowfall,
a film crew, dressed for a picnic, coaxes a peacock
to the chilled street. Six men on their knees
chirruping, laughing, snow lifting in puffs
from the spotlights. And the peacock,
shanks and yellow spurs high-stepping, high-stepping,
slowly unfolds its breathless fan, displays
to a clamor of boxcars, club cars—

where riders, excited,
traveling for miles with an eyeful of bones
see now their reversal.

...
In an ecstasy of color the peacock dips,
revolves to the slow train:
each rider pressed to a window,
each round face courted in turn.

Mirror

Before the mirror, water gave it
back, the brown surface of another's eye . . .

It is High South Africa, 1630.
Rabbles of sailors press down the Zambezi.
Now, strewn out through their empty camp:
burlap, fig stones, and this—
this oblong, black-backed glass.

Clear night. The first creep in
from the bushwood, sifting.
This is my face, one whispers. A flush
like a thud in the brain. *This is my face,
unrippled. Its pockets and stains. Its long
surprise.*

A mynah calls in her seven voices:
Aye   Aye   Aye   Aye . . .

Something lifts up through the mangroves.
Something sets in.

Tongue

I did not know that my fingers were spelling
a word, or even that words existed.

—HELEN KELLER

Imagine another,
blind, deaf since birth.
One, nearly two, she squats at the lip
of a shallow pond. Above her,
the day exchanges its sunlight, clouds.
This she feels in blushes across her shoulders.

With a sleepwalker's grope
she is reaching, patting the cold grasses,
and now, from a tangle of water cardinals
she has plucked a pond-snail. Moist and shell-less

it sucks across her palm.
Tongue, she senses, the simile
wordless, her fingers tracing the plump muscle,
the curling tip.
Someone approaches. To the bowl
of her free hand, the name is spelled,
the tingling *sn* and *ail.*
Again. Again.

And soon she will learn. The naming.
The borders of self,
other. But for now, propped in the musky
shoregrass, it is tongue she senses,

as if the snail, mute, in the lick
of its earthy foot,
contained a story. As if her hand
received it.

Child in the Wagon

The child in the wagon remembers a sound:
leaves that clicked down the cobblestones
like the toenails of running dogs.
It was evening. She turned, expecting the worst,
and found instead the swirl of madrona leaves
and then on the street corner
candle flames cupped in their glass boxes.

It will not hear that sound again, she thinks,
and looks to her left, right,
where the long Conestoga wagons bumble
through the switchgrass. There are forty, indigo
and red, moving not single file but *abreast*,
their hoops and canvas hoods swaying white, and
seen from above, the child thinks, like a wave
spilling into the harbor, its line of froth
and the dust swelled up behind like a second wave.

So the pattern continues, until day ends
and the center wagons stall, all their horses
simply stepping in place as the end wagons
arc toward one another and the wagoners
on their lazyboards draw up
their perfect circle, like the nets of Maine fishermen.
That evening, near sleep on the floorboards,
the child describes to her parents
the sound of madrona leaves, running dogs.
How, for an instant, fear passed through her
like an icy tooth—the long-haired sea dogs
rushing in from the ships—
and then there was nothing: leaves, a certain peace.

...

And that sound . . . like this? her mother whispers,
clicking knives to a pewter cup. Then the father—
who will die in October, his cheeks in miniature
the caved salt cliffs they are leaving—
begins, tapping this, that, this, that,
until the wagon, in its circle of wagons, fills.
And there on the canvas, the child thinks,
how beautiful the hand shadows are:
great moths come in from the wilderness.
Like this? they ask. Like this?
As if in a moment, the absolute sound
might appear—then the dogs rush past, thick with loss.
And there would be peace.

Pearl

First the skip stutters down its rail-line
and the miners, stacked together, knee to knee-back,
stomach to buttock, watch
the clouds, one Douglas fir, a V-tip
of station roof, condense, condense, until
everything they have walked through is a little moon
shining one hundred, one thousand feet,

and exchanged now, from below, for a sparkle
of dusty headlamp—
its growth, like a moon, then
the face and great-boots.

It is always raining. Always
the temperature of sliced ham cooled on a platter,
a placemat, these things of another world.
And unfolded, the miners step into their day, which is
night, walking behind one another
out through the drift tunnels.
An ore cart wobbles by, steaming
with quartz rubble, a little gold perhaps,
the size of a thumbnail, pushed up
from the earth's molten center, through the molten veins,
pushed and pushed—the great pressure, great heat—
to this exact intersection of
vertical, horizontal. . . .

Ears pop.
Someone is singing. And beyond,
from another chamber, comes the whistle of nitrate
billowing up from its spitter fuse.

Now and then some tremble may continue, up
through the ankles, thighs. There is the wheeze
of a bank collapsing, and into the drift tunnel

creep the poisons of powder fumes, methane.
It is then, with the motion of bathers, that
the miners dip into their airmasks, bite
down, and turn together, all
the headlamps reversing their light

to its first horizon.
And nothing can stop what follows,
not science, not the elements:

in a grave interaction of chemicals, saliva,
the airmask biteplates begin heating.
Past the mulch and black-slush, into the skip,
up through the timbers, they grow hotter,
hotter, scorching the tongue,
the palate, until the miners, trapped by a halo
of methane, by the slow pull
of the skip-cable, feel their hearts withdraw, feel
their nerves collect in this new center, foreign
and not—all the flames pushing off,
regathering—the great heat, great pressure—
foreign and not.
But for their eyes, these workers are the color of
quartz rubble, stacked
and lifted . . . lifting . . . past the shale beds,
limestone, from the rain into the rain . . .
and here is that moon, swelling to meet them—
old ghost, old platter of steam—
and here is the world of the world.

Reviving the Geyser:
Reykjavík, Iceland, 1935

—from a photograph by Jon Dahlman

One man in a derby hat, another
in leggings, and a woman
with the brown, sensible shoes of a chemist.
Just behind these friends
is a thermal circle of
dwarf willow, eyebright, and heath—
and before them, the slack basin,
no hiss and bellow, no steam
hurling up its magnificent stitch.

There is urgency on these faces.
Already the snows creep
closer to this mild setting,
like a ringmaster's animals.

To encourage pressure, the man
in the derby hat drops
chunks of pan soap through the quiet water.
They sink like yellow skulls,
and then on the surface

he sees the rippling legs of the woman,
his own small face in its black topknot.
A woodcock sings from a tangle of willow.
The man thinks of his wife at the loom, how
often in the late, thin light her beautiful arms
cross and recross the breast beam

...
with the strokes of a swimmer.
There is pain in his shoulders, in
his pale neck stretched
over the basin. He thinks of a time
when love, in terms of
his place in the world, was everything.

Erebus

Even in the rigging there is chaos,
the foremast and mainmast square-rigged,
the mizzenmast and jibs fore-and-aft-rigged, so their lines
cut in at slants, sharp and terrifying,

like the slant-lights of the Scriptures.

And their flurry is extended to the deck,
where snow curls up with the chocks.
By midnight the waterbuckets freeze, each claiming
at dawn a wafer of thumbskin, peeled back

from its slick under-mate like the eyelids of the dying.
We are just below forty now: Franklin, Fitzjames,
the surgeons, ice-master, thirty seamen, and cook.
And a small bird the color of celadon,
of the hummocks and fog-green fjords stumbling
off from the shoreline. It carries just under a wing
a circle of fuchsia down, blinking out
now and then like our lost sun.

Northwest Passage! Not even a harbor. Barrow Strait,
Boothia, Cape Felix. And the days are lessening.
We inch to the south as the icebergs themselves inch off
from the main-pack: the crack and rustle,
the slow letting go.

What world is this that tightens under us—
each time the wind recedes, freezes
under us, leaving just our small bouquet
of masts and grindstones, a hogshead of sugar?

...
Now and then, ice-locked in this awkward
and constant half-light, we walk over the floes,
watch the simple flight-strokes of snow bunting,

then carry their image to our own companion.
It washes its wings in cabin air.
As the fuchsia circle blinks out, again and again,
we practice our game of resemblances, creeping
closer to all we have been:

God's eye, someone offers. Or ember.
Raw thumb! A taffeta underskirt.
Or a blossom a bullet might leave,
on its journey to a darker harbor.

From the Ghost, the Animal

—Of all the figures in delirium tremens,
the most common is the gray dog.

Not the rat, then. We assumed it was the rat,
scratching up not hell exactly, but
the path there. We assumed
it was the spider, leech,
each in from its Gothic other, those zones
with us and not, like sleep.

But the dog, gray dog—
flock-guider, companion for the slow
rowing—pads in from the hallway,
your life in tow.
                    And please,
there is something wrong with the light,
this muzzle, honed to a trowel,
its jab, retreat, this
dirge through a smile of froth. Up
from your ribs, lungs, up
from the hollows you walk through—

wind, black shoe, the sun at your eyelids,
the simple bread—up from the ghost
and the animal, you answer—bellow,

hideous whine—while he slumps to the floorboards,
clear-eyed, pants *Run*
with me, darling, the meadows, the lost day.

Wonders

In a wide hoop of lamplight, two children—
a girl and her younger brother—jump marbles
on a star-shaped playboard. Beside them,
in a chair near a window, their father
thinks of his mother, her recent death

and the grief he is trying to gather.
It is late October. The hooplight spreads
from the family, through the window,
to the edge of a small orchard, where
a sudden frost has stripped the fruit leaves
and only apples hang, heavy and still
on the branches.

The man looks from the window, down
to a scrapbook of facts he is reading.
The spider is proven to have memory, he says,
and his son, once again, cocks his small face
to the side, speaks a guttural oh, as if
this is some riddle he is slowly approaching,
as if this long hour, troubled with phrases
and the queer turn in his father's voice,
is offered as a riddle.

There is the sound of marbles
in their suck-hole journeys, and the skittery
jump of the girl's shoe
as she waits, embarrassed, for her father
to stop, to return to his known self, thick
and consistent as a family bread.
But still he continues,

...
plucking scraps from his old book, old
diary of wonders: the vanishing borders
of mourning paper, the ghostly shape
in the candled egg, beak and eye
etched clearly, a pin-scratch of claw.

A little sleet scrapes at the window.
The man blinks, sees his hand on the page
as a boy's hand, sees his children bent over
the playboard, with the careful pattern
of their lives dropping softly away, like
leaves in a sudden frost—how the marbles
have stalled, heavy and still on their fingers,
and after each phrase the guttural
oh, and the left shoe jumping.

Lesson: The Spider's Eighth Eye

These three things then: They have eight eyes.
They have memory. Their images do not overlap.

They leave the brood-cocoon when the last grains
of yolk rattle in their pearly bellies.
Each climbs a blade of grass, a twig,
a splintering fence . . . anything sharp and solitary.
Here they send a thread-hook for the wind.

The launch is terrifying: Whipped to a current,
gusted, their legs sucked behind at first
like so much hair. But somehow they shinney,
and they ride those gossamer V's like arrowheads.

This process—the launch, the travel—this is
called ballooning. Some balloon for days.
They are often found in a ship's rigging
hundreds of miles from shore.
Or matting an airplane windshield, like cloud-frays.
Those who survive live their lives where the current
drops them. They do not balloon again.

Now, finally, the eyes. They can not converge.
One pair may see you—not as a face, exactly,
but a pale avoidance—just as another sees
the mantel tray, like a gold sun
without heat or shadow.

The eighth eye is tucked below, and has a range
no higher than your knee. It sees only floors,
soil, crackles of plaster. It is the memory eye.

Sometimes when a draft gusts under the door,
or wind whisks the porch, the eighth eye remembers.
It is all very fast—just a spark, in fact:

The wide rush of sea, perhaps a few whales below,
like sun-spots. And then the great, flapping
net of a sail.

Of course, the wind should be very brisk.
But since there is memory,
this is how it must be.

The Anatomy Lesson of Dr. Nicolaas Tulp: Amsterdam, 1632

High winter. All canals
clogged with an icy marrow. And the flax—
just a blue wash in the mind of
the painter who puffs up the tower stairs.
It is the time for festival—Aris Kindt
is hanged. And soon

up through these same stairs, up
to the slope-seated deal and chestnut
Theatrum Anatomicum, the surgeons will come:
Mathys and Hartman, Frans, Adriaan,
three Jacobs, then the bleeders and barbers,
the wheelwrights, needle-makers, goldsmiths,
the potters and sculptors, two
thin-chested harehounds. A lesson!
A dissection! All the reverent, mercantile faces
peering off through the scaffolds

that are now just empty,
just a deal and chestnut funnel tapered down
to a corpse:
        Aris Kindt. Quiver-maker.
One necklace of rope-lace curled under his ears—
while over his body, the shadow of a painter's hat
circles, re-circles, like a moth at a candle.

So this is fresh death, its small, individual teeth.

Rembrandt walks past the breechcloth, then the forearm
soon to split to a stalk that would be grotesque

but for its radiance: rhubarb tendons
on a backdrop of winter. He swallows,
feels the small dimplings of lunch pork

drop away. And here will be Tulp,
his tweezers and white ruff. And here,
perhaps Hartman, perhaps the shadow of
a violet sleeve closing over the death-face.
It is commissioned: eight faces
forever immortal, and one—slightly waxen—
locked in mortality! He smiles.
How perfect the ears, and the pale eyelids

drawn up from the sockets
like the innerlids of pheasants. Just outside a window,
the day has climbed down to the amber color
of this candlelit room. Rembrandt turns,
crosses out past the sponges and vessels.
There is the sputter of wagon wheels through a fresh ice,
and in all the storefronts
torches hang waiting for a pageant—

scarlet blossoms for a new spring.

His room has turned cold with the slow evening.
Far off in a corner
is a canvas clogged with the glue-skin of rabbits—a wash
of burnt umber, and the whites
built up, layer by layer.
Now a fire, the odor of beets.
And here, where the whites buckle, will be Tulp,
perhaps Mathys, their stunned
contemplation of death. He touches a spoon,
...

then a curve of plump bread. All across his shoulders
and into his hairline winds a little chill,
thin and infinite, like a thread-path
through the stars:
                              there will be umber
and madder root, yellow ocher, bone-black,
the scorch of sulfur, from
the oils of walnut and linseed—all things of the earth—
that forearm, that perfect ear.

Zuni Potter: Drawing the Heartline

Through the scratch-strokes of piñon, the hissing
arroyos, through the clamped earth
waxed and swollen,
coil to coil, paddle to anvil,
the bowl on her palm-skin blossoms,
the bowl on her lap
blossoms, the lap blossoms

in its biscuit of bones.
Bract-flower, weightless, in the pock and shimmer
of August, she slopes from the plumegrass like
plumegrass. And the white skull
bobbles and turns. The gingerroot fingers
turn. Through the cocked mouth
of a buck deer, she sketches an arrow,
its round path nostril to heart.
For the breath going in.
For the breath going out.
Wind to heartbeat. The blossoms of steam.

Wedding

—from the painting by Jan van Eyck

Wait. The groom stops,
right hand in mid-air, mid-ceremony,
about to descend to the cupped right hand
of the bride. What is that noise?
At their feet, the ice-gray griffin terrier stops.
Two puff-shouldered witnesses just entering
the chamber, just entering the scene
through the iris of a convex mirror,
stop. And follow a curling sight-path
from the elegant to the natural: from the dangling
aspergillum and single ceiling candle, down,
past the groom's velvet great-hat, his Bordeaux robe,
past the stiff-tailed lapdog, the empty
crow-toed wooden sandals, to
a trail of yellow apples—desk, ledge, windowsill

and out. *There.* Below. It is
the rasp of water casks on the hunt mares, squeezed
stave pin to stave pin, as
they are shouldered across the canal bridge. And the mares—
how brilliant in the high sunlight:
one roan, one walnut, eight legs
and the rippling ankles rippling again
where the slow Zwin passes under. In a moment

they will cross, step on with their small cargoes
past inns, the great cloth halls steaming with linens.
The mudflats have dried now. All their patterns

of fissures and burls like the rim
of a painter's palette. Once or twice
the cones of yellow flax straw will flicker,
the autumn birch leaves flicker,
the mares lurch left, then

right themselves—nothing to fear after all: not wind, motion.
Not even a sleeve of sackcloth slipped over the hoof.
To quiet the hunt. To make from its little union
not a predator, but a silence.
Just the half-light of forests, black leaves
on their withered stems,
then the graceful, intricate weave closing over
the mossy sole—as a hand might be closed
by a descending hand,
pale, almost weightless, and everywhere.

The Klipsan Stallions

Just one crack against the sandbar
and the grain freighter crumbled into
itself like paper in flames, all the lifeboats
and blankets, the tons of yeasty wheat
sucked down so fast the tumbling sailors

still carried in the flat backs of their brains
the sensations of the galley, smoky with mutton fat,
someone's hiccup, someone's red woolen sleeve
still dragging itself across their eyes

even as the long sleeve of the water closed over them.

It was 3 a.m., the third of November, 1891.
Just to the south of this chaos, where the Columbia
washes over the Pacific,

there was shouting, the groan of stable doors,
and over the beachfront, a dozen
horses were running. Trained
with a bucket of timothy to swim rescue,
they passed under the beam of the Klipsan lighthouse,
passed out from the grasses, alfalfa,
deep snores and the shuffle of hooves,

and entered the black ocean.
Just heads then, stretched nostrils and necks
swimming out to the sailors
who were themselves just heads, each brain
a sputtering flame above the water.
Delirious, bodies numb, they answered

the stallions with panic —
So this is the death parade, Neptune's
horses lashed up from Akasha!
                              And still,
through some last act of the self, when
the tails floated past they grabbed on,

then watched as the horses
returned to themselves, as the haunches
pulled, left then right, and the small circles
of underhooves stroked up in unison. Here
was the sound of sharp breathing, troubled
with sea spray, like bellows left out in the rain,
and here the texture of sand on the belly,
on the shirt and thigh, on the foot
with its boot, and the naked foot — and then, finally,
the voices, the dozens gathered to
cheer the rescue, the long bones of the will,
causing hands to close over those rippling tails,
yellow teeth to close over the timothy.

Mid-Plains Tornado

I've seen it drive straw straight through a fence post—
sure as a needle in your arm—the straws all erect
and rooted in the wood like quills.
Think of teeth being drilled, that enamel and blood
burning circles inside your cheek. That's like the fury.
Only now it's quail and axles, the northeast bank
of the Cedar River, every third cottonwood.

It's with you all morning. Something wet in the air.
Sounds coming in at a slant, like stones
clapped under water. And pigs, slow to the trough.
One may rub against your leg, you turn with a kick
and there it is, lurching down from a storm cloud:
the shaft pulses toward you across the fields
like a magician's finger.
You say goodbye to it all then, in a flash over
your shoulder, with the weathervane so still
it seems painted on the sky.

The last time, I walked a fresh path toward the river.
Near the edge of a field I found our mare, pierced
through the side by the head of her six-week foal.
Her ribs, her great folds of shining skin,
closed over the skull. I watched them forever, it seemed:
eight legs, two necks, one astonished head curved
back in a little rut of hail. And across the river
slim as a road, a handful of thrushes set down
in an oak tree, like a flurry of leaves
drawn back again.

Strike

First the salt was removed,
then the axes and powderhorns,
the blankets, jerky, shot-pouches, gourds,
the kettles and muslin, the burlap torsos of
cornmeal, and the wagons hauled on the coil of rope,
hand over hand, up
the last granite face of the High Sierra,
dangling, wobbling fat in that wind like lake bass,

then the oxen, pushed up the spidery trail —
in the concave crooks of their shanks,
the mules, centered and pushed —

and then it was all restored.

Soon the nut pines yielded to scrub pines, the wind
to the screams of the handcarts —
wooden axles, wooden wheel hubs,
day after day, the haunting, wooden voices.

Now and then, the lowland flashed up
through the trees, russet and gold-filled:
Ophir, Mineral Bar, the American River. Then
the scrub pines gave way to the black oaks, the wistful
manzanitas. On the bank of a river-fork
someone knelt, pinched the gravel,
plump and auriferous. Two others
talked of their journey, and the journey
of gold, of their last descent and that climbing:
fold-fault and lifting, erosion,

glaciation, explosion,
the magma and silica scratching upward,

pin-step by pin-step to meet them.
All night the rain washed over the wagons,
cut down through the wheel ruts and fire-pits,
the powdery topsoil, as if to say
Deeper, just a little deeper,
and in the morning, pulled up in the muzzles
of mules, dangling in the grassy root-tips,
that gold dust, that ending.

FROM *Heart and Perimeter* (1991)

———

The Shakers

Picture a domino. A six perhaps, or placid
four. And resting upon it, like the grids in some
basement windows, three thin vertical lines.
This is a staff—for the dance notations of Rudolf Laban.
Torso twists, step turns and wrist folds,
gallops, jumps, all the motions
a body might make—in space, in time—
contractions, rotations, extensions, from head tilt
to the crook of the left thumb's outer segment,

spatter the staff in symbols. Black dots
and miniature boxcars, tiny rakes
for the fingers, double crosses for the knees,
the right ear's sickle, the eyebrow's mottled palette,
each intricate sketch on its half inch of grid line—
until a string of speckled rectangles

might tell us a foot was lifted,
set down at a slant on the metatarsus,
as a man might step down a path of loose stones.
In the late-morning light, on the road to New Lebanon,
his elbow jumps with its bucket of lake bass.
Now and then, a whistle begins, spreads
into song, then the slack-cheeked slip into piety.

By midday his movements are rhythmic,
have become this dance passed down
through the centuries, then trapped in a patchwork
of labanotation. Two circles: one men, one women.
Stage left, a singer, a pulse of percussion.
The music begins and the circles are carriage wheels,

then closer—almost touching—are the black-specked wheels
of a gear: one men, one women, in turn almost

touching, then the arms flung up in denial,
the bodies flung back into rippling lines,
fused, yet solitary, like a shoal of lake bass.
If there were lanterns then, they are lost here,
and smoke, the odors of sawdust, linseed.
But the costumes are true—white bibs and transparent
skullcaps, each foot in its column of black boot—

and the dancers strive with an equal devotion,
as if the feat of exact repetition were a kind of
eternity. Black dots and miniature boxcars.
Step here, they say, just here. And a foot is lifted,
a quick smile answers, This is enough, this striving—

daylight as it is with its sudden rain,
all the pockets of loose stones glistening.

For the Sake of Retrieval

As Whistler heard colors like a stretch of music —
long harmonies, violet to amber, double hummings of
silver, opal — so, in reverse, these three in their capsule,

free falling two hours through the black Atlantic, ears
popped, then filled with the music of Bach or Haydn,
might fashion a landscape. Low notes bring
a prairie perhaps, the sharps a smatter of flowers,
as the pip notes of sonar spring back to the screen
in little blossoms. They have come for the lost *Titanic*

and find instead, in the splayed beam of a headlamp,
silt fields, pale and singular, like the snow fields
of Newfoundland. On its one runner blade the capsule slides,
slips out through drift hummocks, through
stones the Ice Age glaciers dropped, its trail
the foot-thin trail of a dancer, who
plants, glides, at his head the flurry

of a ship's chandelier, at his back a cinch-hook of icebergs
cast down through the winds of Newfoundland.
The music these three absorb
stops with the wreckage, with words
lipped up through a microphone:
flange, windlass, capstan, hull plating, then oddly, syllables
at a slant, as light might slant through window slats,

stairsteps, doorknob, serving bowl, teacup, Bordeaux.
Mechanical fingers, controlled by the strokes
of a joy stick, brush over debris, lifting, replacing.
In jittery strobe lights, camera lights, all colors

ground down to a quiet palette,
angles return, corners and spirals
pull back to the human eye—as if from some

iced and black-washed atmosphere, boiler coal,
a footboard and platter, each common shape
brightened, briefly held for the sake of retrieval.
The current spins silt like a sudden storm.
With the intricacy of a body the capsule adjusts,
temperature, pressure. Someone coughs, then the three

sit waiting, as in Whistler's *Sad Sea*
three are waiting. All around them are dollops
of winter wind, everywhere beach and sea. No horizon
at all in this painting, just a grey/brown thrum
beach to sea. How steady his breath must have been
on the canvas, his hands on the brushstrokes
of lap robes, of bonnets and beach chairs, the pull
of a red umbrella: each simple shape
loved and awash in the landscape.

April

A little wind. One creak from a field crow.
And the plow rips a shallow furrow, hobbles
from guide-stake to guide-stake,
draws its first contour line,
and parallel, its next, next,
then the turn-strips and deadfurrows, the headlands
and buffer lines, until the earth from a crow's vantage
takes the pattern of a fingertip.

And by noon the shadows are gridways: cut soil,
the man on the plow, the plow and simple tail,
each squat on a stretch of slender shade,
black and grid-straight, like the line of anti-light

a screen clicks up to, before its image
swells, deepens. Dark glass
going green, in the shade-darkened room
of a laboratory—it casts a little blush
across the face there, the shoulders and white pocket,
then magnifies the moon-skin of a microbe, then deeper,
electron molecules in a beam so stark it smolders.

The man on the plow fears frost,
its black cancer. The man at the screen
fears the storm an atom renders
on the lattice of a crystal. And heat. And the slick
back-licks of vapor. With luck, with the patience
the invisible nurtures, he will reshape

frost-making microbes, snip frost-hook genes
with a knife of enzymes. And at thirty degrees,

twenty, through seam lines of snap beans, oranges,
almonds, potatoes, no frost will form, no ratchet-bite
of ice, all the buds of transformed microbes
blossoming, reblossoming, like the first flowers.

There is wind at the rim of the black-out shade.
One tick of the focus gears. Another. On a glass plate,
enlarged from nothing to filaments, the lines
of DNA wander, parallel, in tandem,
curled together past pigment blips, resin,
as the contour lines for autumn oranges
swerve in unison past boulder pods. The light

through the mottled skins of genes
is not light at all, but friction, caught and channeled,
like pigment caught in the scratch-marks of caves.
This was our world, the marks say: horse, maize,
vast gods drawn down to a palm print.
Drawn up from nothing the microbes gather,
a little wind on the curtain,
sun on the curtain's faded side, on the crow and plow,
on the earth sketched perfectly to receive it.

Ringing

This thimble one, with a lentil clapper.
This one of shell.
These top-notched ones, for the harnesses of horses.
And these, for the fist-shaped, candle-spun
carousels of children. This one of the pear-shape,
this of the tulip, the fish mouth, the pomegranate,
the beehive. This room-sized one, stung
by four men in black braids, their arms
underhanding a muted log, in unison,
underhanding, casting the sanded log-tip
to the lotus-etched sweet-spot of the bell,
then again, underhanding in unison, like
the casters of waterbuckets, the ring and the splay,

and slowly, the child closes her book. A sound
has begun, just out from the window. A tap-scratch,
thwirr. Some rabbit, perhaps, trapped
in a shallow snare, great hind feet
plucking tufts from the crabgrass. She rises,
sits back in her soft chair, rises. Perhaps she will
witness a certain death, but the shelter of the book
is memory now, the path to the window
infinite, nothing, as she steps, stalls, steps, then
slips shoulder first to the waxy pane—and there
is her brother in the orchard below, casting stones
with a sling through the dense, brittle leaves
of the sugar maples. No targets at all there, no prey—

his small head tipped and attentive—just the pull,
release, then, long after, the answerings.

Bird in Space: First Study

—Constantin Brancusi

Nothing grows in the shadow of great trees . . .
And yet, in a wine cask's shadowy tube—oak aged
and curved to a first-growth trunk—
his legs inched up from his ankles.
He was sixteen, alone. By a storefront window
in Craiova, great breaths of chocolate
sighing out from a churn stick

held him. And the pattern of wheat dust
on silos, the pattern of corn
on a pulpy cob, like the grid marks in squid.
Hunger. Its spidery grip. And then he was hired,
dipped by the wrists into wine casks.
Small, slender—the restaurant above him
no more than a wind of garlic—he lathered, scrubbed,

all the pips slipping out from the rough-hewn wood,
all the bristle tips, esters,
and the odors of yeast, wet wool, the wine sludge
curved to the shape of his knees, his fingertips
curved to the oak blebs: body and barrel
in equal exchange—a melding, a kiss.

Days passed. A year. Often at dusk
he read cards at the restaurant tables, watched
the wide Rumanian faces swell, withdraw.
From the circle of Chariots, of Towers
and delicate Hanged Men, a fear would begin,

brushing up through each face like a wine flush.
Enigmas. The queer burbles of candle wax.
Then a cello spun out its long notes, binding,
cupping them all to the known earth,

as, morning by morning, the slats of an oak wine cask
cupped his small body. Sometimes
he sang there—cello songs, drawn down to the tempo
of bristle tips, splinters. Sometimes he studied
his hoop-slice of sky: looped from the ceiling, from
strings like the rays of geometry, amber onions,
three halved by the barrel rim's sharp circumference,
beets and beet tufts, and, weekly,

the marbled hind legs of a roebuck.
Globe shapes, light-polished, or cragged
by a smatter of earth. Then weekly,
arcing into his view from a fuller body,
two thighs, two hocks, pulled tight at the hooves
by a thread of rawhide: pale form in a fixed arc,
like the memory of motion, like a bird stalled
in the ice-winds of space, its stillness, flight.

White Bears:
Tolstoy at Astapovo

The wheels of the train were a runner's heartbeat—
systole, diastole, the hiss-tic of stasis—
as they flipped through the scrub trees and autumn grasses,
slowing at last at the station lamps.
And perhaps the fever had carried this memory,
or the journey, or, just ahead in the darkness,
the white, plump columns of lamplight.

He is five, six, locked at the center
of the evening's first parlor game:
*Go stand in a corner, Lyova, until you stop thinking
of a white bear.* To his left,
there is pipe smoke. Behind him
a little laughter from the handkerchiefs.
And in his mind, white fur
like the blizzards of Tula! He studies the wall cloth
of vernal grass and asters, a buff stocking, trouser cuff,
but just at the rescue of a spinet bench
two claws scratch back. A tooth. Then
the lavender palate of polar bears.

I cannot forget it, he whispers. And would not,
through the decades that followed—
the white, cumbersome shape
swelling back, settling, at the rustling close
of an orchard gate, or the close
of a thousand pen-stroked pages,

white bear, in the swirls of warm mare's milk,
at the side of the eye. White bear,

when his listless, blustery, aristocratic life
disentangled itself, landlord to
shoemaker, on his back a tunic, in his lap
a boot, white bear, just then,
when his last, awl-steered, hammer-tapped peg
bit the last quarter sole.

In the gaps between curtains. And now,
in the lamp-brightened gaps between fence slats,
there and there, as if the bear
were lurching at the train's slow pace,
and behind it—he was certain—the stifling life he fled
rushing to meet him: family, servants, copyrights,
just over the hill in the birch trees.
Simplicity. He sighed. Dispossession.
A monastery, perhaps. Kasha in oil. At eighty-two,
his body erased to the leaf-scrape of sandals.
And even the room near the station, the small bed
with its white haunch of pillow,

even the mattress, where he shivered
with fever or a train's slow crossing, and whispered,
and, just before morning, died,
was better. Deep autumn. Already the snows
had begun in the foothills, erasing
the furrows and scrub trunks, erasing at last
the trees themselves, and the brooks,
and the V-shaped canyons the brooks whittled.
There and there, the landscape no more
than an outreach of sky, a swelling, perhaps,
where an orchard waited, then boundary posts, fence wire,
then, below, the lavender grin of the clover.

In the Beeyard

Clover-rich, lugged close to the thorax and twirring heart,
wax-capped, extracted, the viscid liquid
is not gold at all, but the color of cellophane, ice.
A little heat and its sugars may darken,
emerge, as fingerprints rise through a dusting of talcum,

but there in the dry-packed winter beehives
it is clear, the complex nothing of air or water.
And warm—although the orchard outside has slowly chilled,
snow on the windbreak, deep snow on the hives
in their black jackets. The honey is warm,
and the hive walls, and the domes of bearded wheat straw
tucked under tarpaper rooflines.

To nurture this tropic climate, the bees
have fashioned a plump wheel, clustered body to body
on honey cells, chests clicking out a friction, a heat—
faster, slower, in inverse proportion
to the day's chill—while the hives
keep a stable ninety degrees, warm-blooded

as the keepers who cross through the beeyard.
They move with the high-steps of waders, a man,
his daughter. He clears blown snow from the hive doors.
She lowers her ear to the deep hummings.
Like mummies, she thinks of the cloaked rows, like
ghosts. Then salt pillars, headless horsemen
turned white by some stark moonlight.
In a flurry the images reach her,

•••

their speed almost frightening, splendid,
as if the myths and fables of her life are a blizzard
drawn suddenly to her, drawn suddenly visible
through some brief interaction of
temperature, light. And the day itself then
swells a half-step closer: the sky and knotted
peach trees, her father's thick form
smelling slightly of bacon. He turns
and a bowed ear blooms, backlit a moment
by the sudden sunlight, little veins and spiderings
plum-colored, then fuchsia, as a warmth spreads
over his face, her shoulders, over the windbreak
and hive doors. She opens her jacket and soft liner.
The bees, in their perfect circle, still.

Nancy Hanks Lincoln in Autumn: 1818

Thirst. And the slow pains of the stomach.
Her heart gives the sound of an oar through water, blunt
and diminishing, or the slipping of hooves over oak roots.

No window in view, yet the door near her bed
frames the nut trees and sycamores, the cows
folded down in a clearing. Like an alchemist's mark
for infinity—loop beside loop, horizontal eight—
each body curls back to itself: shoulder arched, neck dipped,
    head
stretched back to rest on a circle of hip.

Their milk will kill her, their journeys down game paths
to the white, forest blossoms of snake-root.
Bud high with poison, the vine plants rushed,
muzzle, to milk vein, to udder, to a thirst
whose final magnification seems a form of mockery.

An ax claps somewhere to her left. The table
with its belly of puncheon casts the shadow of a ferry,
as if the floor were again the flat Ohio,
Kentucky behind, Indiana just ahead in a chaos of trees.
Someone coughed then, she remembers. Sharp coughs,
skittering. Someone sang of the journey the soul

must make, little boat over water. Their home
took the color of chestnuts. She read aloud
from the fables of Aesop: foxes and eagles. The crow
and the pitcher—its water out of reach,
just off from the tongue, his beak at the rim

•••

like ax strokes. To her left they are chopping,
then whittling a clearing with fire. They are stacking
ripped vines, saplings, and underbrush
like a plump wreath at the base of a sycamore.
It will burn in an arc-shaped heart, huge
and magnificent, dark veins of heat
ripping off at the edges. Will the birds break again then,

out from the trees? The passenger pigeons and parakeets
lift as they have in a thick unit, their thousand bodies
dragging the shadow of a wide pond

down over the game paths, down over the oak trees
and cattle, the doorframe, bedposts, cupped hands,
bellows, the cheese in its muslin napkin?
Until shape after darkened shape floats in a wash of air?

Thirst. Braiding every thought back to an absence.
She drinks from her cup. Drinks again. On a hillside
the children are laughing, called out from their sorrow
by the spectacle of flames. Or by birds
in a sudden jumble, perhaps. Or the placid cows
catching handkerchiefs of ash on their broad faces.
How simply two circles can yield to each other,

curl back to each other without ending:
raised shoulder, a dipping, raised hip.
The path an oar makes in water, in air, then in water.

Träumerei

All I have done in music seems a dream
I can almost imagine to have been real.
—ROBERT SCHUMANN, 1810–1856

Perhaps this, then: the holystone licks
of the winter Rhine. A cleansing.
A scouring away. Anything to free him
from the constant filling.

Weeping, in slippers and dark robe, maddened
by phantom voices, music,
he walks from his house with
the tentative half-steps of a pheasant.
A little rain collects on his robe hem,
and street meal, the cubiform dust-chips
of cobblestones. He has carried no coin purse
and offers to the bridge guard
a silk face cloth, then the image
of a man in bedclothes, in the quarter-arc of flight

from raining to river.
There is wind—upward—
and the parallel slaps of his slippers.
With the abrupt closure of a trumpet mute
his heart stops. Then the music, voices. Water
has flushed through his robe sleeves, and
the thin, peppered trenches
between groin and thigh.

...

He will surface
as an opal surfaces: one
round-shouldered curve of brocade in the wave-chop.
Then his heart kicking back.
And the oarlocks of rowers who are
dipping to save him?
A-notes and A-notes—perfect—in unison.

What else but to starve?
The starched coats of asylum guards
give a fife's chirrups. They are joined by
tintinnabulum, chorus, and oboe
on his brief walks to the ice baths.

At the first flat shocks and frigid clearings
he smiles, murmurs
that his madness is at least his love,
distorted, of course, pervasive, but still . . .
aural. A music. The trees

by the fenceline fill, release. One year,
two. He follows halfway, taking
into the self the quarter-notes of
footsteps, the cacophony of laughter, wagons, doors,
the hums of the candle-snuff.
Writing stops, then speech. No word,
no flagged dot on its spidery stave
to diminish the filling. What else but

to turn from all food, to decrease from without
like the August peaches? To take at the last
the fine, unwavering balance

of an arc—heart and perimeter—
a cup where all sound resonates? . . .

A *bell has fallen in Moscow*, he once wrote,
so huge it carried its belfry to the ground.
And into the ground. The bell lip
and shoulder boring deep in the earth. Then
a cross-rip of belfry. Then, through
the stark reversal of summer grasses,
four pale steps leading down.

The Grandsire Bells

At first quick glance and lingering second,
the five, sludge-smeared miners on the roadway—
through this pre-morning light, with their shock
of canary in its braided cage—
might have seemed to the five ringers approaching

like a portrait of memory, like the sway
and blear of themselves in memory: the bend
of bootsoles in the myrtle grass, black
caps, yellow lantern flame, the knapsack stings
of rhubarb and mildew. And the village

below, coal fires granting to the fresh day
plumes in the fashion of cypresses—base knot,
stalk, the splintering crown-tip—a kind
of memory also, as the ringers trudged
up the hillside, past the miners and smoke strings,

past the fluted iron churchyard fence, the dollops
of marble headstones. Then into the breezeway,
where belfry steps accepted the trudge,
and the bells, above, waited. Five. In a blend
of copper and tin, each shouldered the hub ring

of a great wheel, the bell ropes lashed to spokes
and threaded, the soft-tufted cordage
dangling down to the ringers like a spray
of air roots. With the motion of climbing
the treble was cocked, pulled up to suspend

...

at the balance point, waist and mouth-edge
inverted, hovering. Then the others cocked,
turned up, each ton of fish scale–glistening
arc at rest of a pin-tip of stay.
And toppled. One after one, treble, second,

third, fourth, tenor, toppled. Quick pump and
    spillage,
like heartbeats. Again, the ringers releasing
the strike and hum notes, handstroke to backstroke,
the bells pulled up, up, the snapping ropes wound
up, tail tufts and sally-grips in the jig-play

of dancers. All morning, the swinging
treble wound through its hunt path, a nudge
into second ring, third, fourth, and the second
replacing the tenor bell, and the third knocked
into lead. In the village the day

was a braiding of change-rings, notes swelling,
fading, as the bells turned. In the bracken
and mine shafts. In the foundry, when the forge
bellows hushed and the furnace tapway
spilled a rush of smoking bronze down brick-

lined troughs in the earth floor. Bell notes. When
bronze curled down through buried bell molds, cut
    half-rings
in the earth, cut bell shapes. When the cupped clay
flared and stiffened. Bell notes. Change upon change.
Then ending. Ending. In an instant, closing back

•••

in their first order. All ringers for that second
claiming past, present, like walkers on a roadway:
in the half-light of morning, one shock
of canary in a braided cage,
one curve of lantern flame approaching.

FROM *The Ghost Trio* (1994)

———————

The Winter: 1748

—Erasmus Darwin, 1731–1802

A little satin like wind at the door.
My mother slips past in great side hoops,
arced like the ears of elephants—
on her head a goat-white wig,
on her cheek a dollop of mole.

She has entered the evening, and I
her room with its hazel light.
Where her wig had rested is a leather head,
a stand, perfect in its shadow but
carrying in fact, where the face should be,
a swath of door. It cups

in its skull-curved closure
clay hair stays, a pouch of wig talc
that snows at random and lends to the table

a neck-shaped ring.
When I reach inside I am frosted,
my hand like a pond in winter, pale
fingers below of leaves or carp.

I have studied a painting from Holland,
where a village adjourns to a frozen river.
Skaters and sleighs, of course, but
ale tents, the musk of chestnuts,

...

someone thick on a chair with a lap robe.
I do not know what becomes of them
when the flow revisits. Or why
they have moved from their warm hearthstones
to settle there—except that one step

is a method of gliding,
the self for those moments
weightless and preened as my leather companion.
And I do not know if the fish there
have frozen, or wait in some stasis
like flowers. Perhaps they are stunned
by the strange heaven—dotted with

boot soles and chair legs—
and are slumped on the mud-rich bottom,
waiting through time for a kind of shimmer,
an image perhaps, something
known and familiar, something

rushing above in their own likeness,
silver and blade-thin at the rim of the world.

Memento of the Hours

First the path stones, then the shadow,
then, in a circuit of gorse and mint,
the room with a brook running under it.
It freshened the milk, the cream that grew
in its flat habit a shallow lacquer,
a veil I tested on slow afternoons
with a speckle of pepper.

There was butter, cheddar, the waxy pleats
of squash, green as a storm pond.
Walnuts. Three families of apple,
each with its circle of core fringe.
And the sheen on the walls
was perpetual, like the sheen
on the human body.

My mother would sit with me there,
her drawstring reticule
convex with scent jars and marzipan, the burled
shapes of the hidden. Once she brought her cut
flowers to chill until evening, and told me
the mouths of the bluebells
gave from their nectar a syrup elixir.

It holds in suspension the voices of choirboys,
she said. A dram of postponement.
And I felt as she spoke their presence
among us: the hum
of the brook just under our feet,

the mineral hush of the plenitude,
then the blackened robes of the blackberry vines
gradually filling the door.

Windows

When the cow died by the green sapling,
her limp udder splayed on the grass
like something from the sea, we offered
our words in their low calibrations—
which was our fashion—then severed
her horns with a pug-toothed blade
and pounded them out to an amber
transparency, two sheets that became,
in their moth-wing haze, our parlor windows.
They softened our guests with the gauze-light
of the Scriptures, and rendered to us,
on our merriest days, the sensation
of gazing through the feet of a gander.
In time we moved up to the status
of glass one pane, then two—each
cupping in proof of its purity
a dimple of fault, a form of distortion
enhancing our image. We took the panes
with us from cottage to cottage,
moth-horn and glass, and wedged up
the misfitted gaps with a poultice
of gunny and wax. When woodsmoke
darkened our bricks, we gave
to the windowsills a lacquer
of color—clear blue with a lattice
of yellow: a primary entrance and exit
for light. And often, walking home
from the river and small cheese shop,
we would squint their colors to a sapling
green, and remember the hull
of that early body, the slap of fear

we suffered there, then the little wash
of recovery that is our fashion—how
we stroked to her bones a cadenced droning,
and took back from her absence, our
amber, half-literal method of sight.

The Reversals

Grit metals drawn to a bourbony syrup,
then the tiny ear trumpet is cast: hand-sized
cornucopia, one tendril of head band.
And the child who has followed this process, pickax
to flame, to the small, curved swelling in his day-pouch,
steps off on a mission to the faltering Beethoven,

just as the other, housebound, in a chaos of music sheets
and chamber pots, steps back through his mind
toward Holland. Late autumn. And by noon,
the ice on the deck rails is a lacework of gull prints.
There are waves, unbroken, rolling port to starboard
like a hammock wind. Deep cold. His hands
are made warm by a wrapping of scarf, his feet

by the black drapery of his mother's lap.
Through his frost-fed and wave-rocked drowse,
three nuns on the deck are a gaggle of sea birds,
the arced wings of their huge headpieces
lifting their slender bodies. . . .

Music sheets. Chamber pots. One beckoning
metronome. And the ear trumpets
send off through his nerves
the sensations of a rake scraped over a harp.
Great pipe shapes. Ladles. Just a coolness in the palm,
then a warmth. Or lined up on the tabletop,
an orchestra of reversals, sucking sound
back in, bell to a pucker of mouthpiece.
∎∎∎

A wind has begun in the clear day.
And perhaps they were spirits, there on the deck boards,
a ghostly trio lifting before him—no land
in sight, then his small body so suddenly
his body, so suddenly himself, the hands,
the feet in their soft shoes.

Now a child is standing in the open doorway,
the smallest of ear trumpets shining in his hand:
its perfect walls, the perfect, cupped vessel of it.
Look, he is mouthing, what
has risen from the earth to meet you.

Phantom Pain

—*Josiah Wedgwood, 1795*

It speaks, now and then.
A lisp at the knee. A needle-trill
where the ankle once arced. Then I reach into air
or the concave disturbance of the bedclothes.

And nothing. A pain in an absence. A leg-shaped
absence in pain. I do not know
what it is that calls—
and burns then, unsummoned, like the summer fires
that flame through the bracken.

A low cloud blackens the larch trees.
We have opened the channel through Harecastle Hill
and the vases and flake-white medallions
float down its dark tunnel, the canal boats
slender as fingerlings. No tow path
exists there and the workers must
leg the boats through: propped on their backs
on the cabin rooftops

must stride down that starless ceiling,
not advancing at all, but
advancing all, walking the eggshell jasper bodies
through the dripping darkness.
They tell me the day draws nearer like a lantern,

like the day must arrive
for the climbing colliers: a whiteness

coming closer—but then, as if on the pond
of the inner eye,

the intricate, inverted brilliance of a maple.
A glimpse into heaven, perhaps, or its loss,
the image flicked upright in the questioning mind—
in an instant, already gone
even as it approaches, a form
flaring nearer while backing away.

The Swallows: *1800*

Through the wet and continual trout-chill of earth,
he dropped with his father, past shale beds, black-slush,
down corridors greased with the seeping of springs,
and cranked in the darkness a stuttering flint wheel,
a wand that threw to the pickax and mine walls
quick jitters of light. The sparks left the wheel

in fractured arcs and brought from the darkness
oil slicks, water cans, now and then, a canary
in a wash of anthracite dust, each image
at once arriving, departing, at once

summoned, extinguished. When gasses crept out
through the drift tunnels, the sparks would thicken,
loll at the wheel, flush to the color of rubies, liver,
and be, it seemed, not fire at all, but a wreath
of some alternate element. And before he ran,

pushed by his father—and the other boys
ran with their fathers, calling through the corridors—
he watched at the flint wheel the stopped body
of light, how sparks could be stopped in the shapes
of their bodies, held there, it seemed, forever.

Middays they rested, the axes, the guttural rasps
of the flint wheels, silent. And his father told him
of legends, once of the sparrows of northern nations,
how they gathered by ponds in autumn, joined in a circle
wing to wing, foot to foot, and slowly sank into
the water. How they waited together through winter,

...

long ice pallets forming above them. And the villagers
stooped on the shoreline, watched through the ice
the chestnut bodies, silent in their still circle.
And waited for spring and the sudden rising,
the small birds breaking together to the yellow day.

But how could they eat there? he asked his father.
And breathe, with the water pressed over them?

They stopped, then began again with their rising.

In a wreath? As a single body they rose?

That is the story, his father said. Though
we think they rose as sparks.

Hunter

Plume-shaped and pampered, the flames
at the sitting room hearth are the color
of foxes: sharp amber
dropping down to a sobering port.
It is evening. A boy, Charles Darwin,
having listened as the undertaker's workfellows
removed from the sickroom the body of his mother—
a little satin like wind at the door—

turns now to his father's voice.
A story: the magnificent ears of musicians.
The young Beethoven, perhaps. How,
from the blindness of a sleeping mask,
he distinguished for his gathered diners
the clacket of forks from the clacket of knives.

A quick rain has begun at the window.
And now the story veers: An uncle once drowned
in the Derwent River, once walked through a night storm
to the storm of the current. And as the water
rises, as his father's voice
approaches this alternate loss,

Charles studies the flames until they are foxes,
until they are called from the covert,
their sharp scent firm on the kale. Red coats
and the watery breeches. Black boots. And the ears
of the horses are cropped back to walnuts,
nubbled and sore—the long foreheads
just sloping away, sloping,
and the great eyes stark in their sockets.

...

A music begins then: deep bay
upon deepening bay, the loping hounds
dark and harmonic . . .
And could the uncle distinguish, his father is asking,
the drops of the storm from the drops
of the river? Just then, with his face
half hidden, half blossoming?

And could Charles distinguish, there in the wing chair,
grief from the story of grief? Or fear? Or love
from the story of love? And turn to it—
the grief, the love—harbor it,

however the story might buffer, whatever the loss?
As the man who stands in a yellow field
and takes to his lips a silent whistle,
and accepts that a sound is traveling, just over
the kale, just over the wind, and accepts
his place in some seamless extension,
even as, in a wave, the singing animal world
turns back to him.

Held

Silent, in the loose-fisted grip
of evening, he sits with his infant daughter
and makes from his face an exaggerated mask,
sorrow or glee, shock, the eyebrows launched
toward the hairline, the trenches of the forehead
darkening, so that she might learn —
following, mimicking — not only correspondence,
but a salvaging empathy.

And often in the chambers and drift tunnels
he gestures with the other miners. Deafened
by the strokes of the widow drills, he
offers that mime-talk, clear as the bell codes
for hoist, for lower. Cheeks drawn, the mouth
a tapered egg. Then he turns

in the lamplight, sees the tunnels
gauzed over with dust, feels
his lungs slowly filling, like the gradual
filling of rain ponds, and presses
the widow drill — named for his absence —
through the blue-black petals of anthracite,
through the bones and root-tips,
the shale-brindled cradle of the dead
and the flowering, as the earth

of the earth breaks away. Three thousand feet.
Four. His lungs slowly filling. But perhaps I am
spared, he wonders. Perhaps I am held
by this alternate world, cupped

...

and eternal. As once, just a boy, he stood
with his mother in the bath light.
Her white slip, the twin pallets
of her earrings. A fog of talcum
turned at the mirror. In joy
she delivered its snow to the air,
shake upon shake, smiling,
drawing from his own small mouth
the stunned, obedient smile of a guest.
Her face. Her arm in its little arc.
As if she were saying This
is the gesture for *always* as
the weightless powder settled upon them.

Westray: *1992*

Then the day passed into the evening,
a sovereign, darkening blue. And
the twenty-six lost miners,
if living at all, knew nothing of the hour:
not the languid canter
of light, or the wind
curled through the hedgerows. Not pain.
Not rage. If living at all then
just this: a worm of black water
at the lower back. At the lungs
two tablets of air.

What is it like there? the broadcaster asked,
his voice and the slow reply
cast down through the time zones of America.

A stillness. All of the families
asleep in the fire station.
And the mineworks pale on the landscape.

What else?
Nothing. Blue lights of police cars.

What else?
Nothing.
Nothing?
. . . The thrum of the crickets.

A thousand files on a thousand scrapers.
A thousand taut membranes called *mirrors*
amplifying the breed-song. A landscape of cupped wings
amplifying the breed-song. A thousand bodies
summoned to a thousand bodies—and the song itself a body,
so in tune with the dusk's warmth
it slows when a cloud passes over.
Today. Tomorrow. In that May Nova Scotia darkness
when the earth flared and collapsed.
Before that May. After that darkness.
On the larch bud. On the fire station.
On shale and the grind-steps of magma.
On the gold straining in its seam bed.
On the coal straining. On the twenty-six headlamps
swaying through the drift tunnels. On the bud.
On the leaves, on the meadow grass,
on the wickerwork of shrubs:
dark cape of desire.

call forth from the evening some
celestial repetition of our shared churnings.

We shattered the spout
with shotguns that kicked like the guns of my childhood
when leaves were a prune-mulch and my sisters
stood at the rim of the orchard.
Katty. Caroline. Susan. Marianne.
In the temperate wind, their dresses and sashes,
the variegated strands of their hair, were
the nothing of woodsmoke. Steam.

I cannot foretell our conclusion.

But once, through a pleat-work of waves,
I watched as a cormorant caught and released
a single fish. Eight times. Trapped and released.
Diving into an absence, the fish
re-entered my vision in segments, arcing
through the pivot of the bird's beak. Magnificent,
I thought, each singular visit, each
chattering half-step from the sea.

Six in All

Preface

Across the buckled, suck-hole roads,
my cousin, Mathew Brady's aide, bobbed
toward our scattered camp, his black-robed,
darkroom "whatsit wagon"—its pling
of glass plate negatives—half hearse, half cloaked
calliope. The Civil War was undeveloped
and camp was thick with families, the fields
a hail of slumping tents, their canvas cupping
counterpanes, quilts with hubs of rising sun.

He posed us near our tent's propped flap,
Father, Mother, my toddler sister cupped over
my hip, then waved us to a sudden freeze—
except for Jane, whose squirms became a handkerchief
or dove wing on the ether plate. He took
my father, stiff against the summer larch,
then Mother's ragged silhouette—the two of them,
and us again, and Jane asleep. Six in all,
my family and a chronicle of passing light,
the day by half-steps slipping down
across our hair and collarlines.

In later years, the war long cold, he found
in surplus its brittle song: long rooms
of glass plate negatives, with lesser ones,
he told me—the sunken corpse, the sunken soldier
sipping tea—revived as greenhouse windows.
The houses are magnificent, glass rows of amber
apparitions, that disappear, he said, when rains

begin. That melt, for human eyes at least, into
a kind of nothingness. Then only metal frames
are seen, square by empty square,
like netting on the land.

I would find our family, he said, across
one building's southern wall,
where tandem trunks of windblown oak
arc toward hothouse limes . . .

Six in All

One

From balsa's weightless wood my father carved
the horse, then smoothed it to a foal,
then further still, into a kind of moon — horse yet,
and yet the head in soft relief was lunar, undefined —

as his is now, within the greenhouse wall. Erased
by my cousin's breath, perhaps, upon the plate, across
the damp collodion — his sigh or hum, some humanness
that hovers still, between my father's collarline
and globes of hothouse limes.

Two years beyond this negative, my father drowned
off Georgia's shore — so twice was slain by breathing.
They say on death the lungs accept the sea, inhale
its foreign element, the way I think the shutter's mouth
draws time inside to timelessness.

Before he died, he wrote that flocks of braying mares
were dropped by sling from battleships to waiting scows,
their stiffened legs like canes, he said,
the flashing cane-tips of their hooves.

"For those of us on wet-decked scows, a dozen times
they broke the sun, a dozen dust-caked underbreasts
cast their quick eclipse . . ."

And did I recall our balsa foal? From rye and fern,
from loops of waxy thread, how we wove her green arena?

"God, to have that footing now! — turf instead of
sickly sea, that swings me like some sling-strung beast."

Within the plate glass negative, he waits
near summer larch: boots sharp, coat sharp, but face
dissolved to white. Across the plate's transparent sky,
the hothouse air has spawned an emerald scum,
a silken vegetation that spreads
its spidered reach. He stands below, coat sharp,
boots sharp, his head dissolved to cloud.
It will support him soon, the green.

The Three Trees

Late day. A wash of claret at the window.
And the room swells with the odor of quince,
tin-sharp and dank, as the acid creeps down
through the etch marks. He dips the foreground languidly,
Rembrandt, so thickets will darken, the horse
and lovers resting there, the bamboo latitude
of fishing pole, the shadowed river.

Then inks it all—mixed sky, three dappled trees—
and presses the intricate net of it
to the white-bleached etching sheet below: one skein
of storm aligning the nothingness, one haycart
rich with villagers. At the window now,

a fading to ochre. And beyond,
through the streets and valley, at the base
of a hillock thick with three trees, a hunter
is ringing a treble bell, its quick bite
driving the field birds to the sheltering grasses.
Around him, dark in their earth-colored clothes,
others are throwing a slack-weave net

out over the meadow and scuttering birds.
And up from their various hands, quick fires bloom,
rush through the beard grass, the birds bursting up
to the capturing net, some dying of fright,
some of flames, some snuffed by the hunters

like candles. A breeze begins, slips through the tree limbs.
Slung over each hunter are threadings of birds,
strung through the underbeak. Pleat-works of plenitude,

down the back, the curve of the shoulder.
They offer their warmth in slender lines,
as sunlight might, through the mismatched shutters
of a great room, the long gaps casting

their cross-hatch. As if time itself might spin them all
down some vast, irreversible pathway—
haycart, hunter, small bowl with its blossoms of quince—
and the simple patterns resting there
barred everything back from the spinning.

Altamira: What She Remembered

That, chased by a covey of hunters, the fox
slipped into its den
exactly as bread slipped into her father's mouth:
white with a tapering backstroke of brown.

That the hunters at the den door
chopped and chopped with their black heels.

That the cave they revealed, child-sized but
humid with promise, ticked
with a placid rain, as if the weather
of the sky were the weather of the earth.

That she saw on the cave walls, in blue-black
and ochre, "the bulls," although they were bison,
she learned, and a dipping hind.

That the borders of her body were the borders
of the weather.

That whatever awakened within her there —
not grief, not fear — had the sound
of hooves down a cobbled street.

That they lifted her back by one arm.

That, as she walked with her father
through the downland, the sound of the hooves
settled.

...

That whatever awakened within her there
had the sound of birds
flushed from the downland grasses.

Had the sound of leaves from a pitchfork's tines.

Years later, had the ticking sound of the rain.

Six in All

Two

"Now hold," he said, his bloated word
afloat in the black-cloaked chamber.
And Mother stopped in profile. She had turned
to witness lifting moths, their thrum
across the oaks, then held to watch that tuft of air

that was the moths, empty yet filled
with tracks of the missing, like
the crease her cast-off headscarf left,
crown to milky ear. I stood outside the camera's frame,

near tables fat with yellowed shirts and vats
of crystal vinegar. Beyond the oaks, a soldier
worked against a plow, leaned back across
its harness straps, as if to cancel cultivation,
as if to close the trough that foamed before him.
His uniform was stiffened wool, his shirt fresh blue
against the field: half farmer still, half infantry,
a slanted shape that branched between
two worlds of burial.

My mother swallowed, saw the shutter spiral down,
her face a blend of dust and wonder—
that she might gather over glass, that she might claim,
across the flecks of bromide salt, some bygone self.

The sunlight cast quick glints against the plow,
across the rippling skins of vinegar.
My mother laughed, stepped forward

...

through the grass. Once she penned a note in vinegar's ink—
invisible, but for blisters wetness leaves. Like magic,
she said, how heat will mark each letter's path. Some greeting,

I think, her words so short-lived their birth
was withdrawal. We held the page to a candle's flame
and letters stroked up on mottled wings.
Then "Look," she whispered, "their quickening shapes:
the thumb-plump, the sickled,
the branching-away . . ."

The Geographer

—from the painting by Vermeer

There. Out the window. They are burning the flood fields.
And the light that touches his forehead
is softened by smoke. He is stopped in a long robe,
blue with a facing of pumpkin. In his hand,
the splayed legs of a compass taper to pin tips.

It is noon. Just after dawn, he took
for his errant heart a paper of powdered rhubarb
and stoops to the window now, half in pain, half
in love with the hissing fields:

mile after mile of cane stalks, fattened
with drawn water. Such a deft pirouette, he thinks,
flood pulled up through the bodies of cane, then
water cane burned into steam, and steam like mist
on the fresh fields, sucked dry for the spring planting.

Powdered rhubarb. Like talc on the tongue.
And what of this heart, this blood? Harvey writes
that the washes of pulse do not ebb, do not
flow like the sea, but circle, draw up to the plump heart.
And is that the centering spirit then? Red plum,
red shuffling mole? . . .

When the flood waters crested, the dark coffins
bobbed down through the cane stalks like blunt pirogues.
And then in the drift, one slipper
and the ferreting snouts of radishes.

...

He touches his sleeve, looks down to his small desk,
pale in its blanket of map, all the hillsides
and carriageways, all the sunken stone walls
reduced to the sweep of a pin tip.
They are burning the flood fields—such a hissing, hissing,

like a landscape of toads. And is that how blood
circles back in its journey, like water through
the body of the world? And the great, flapping fire, then—
opening, withering—in its single posture
both swelling and fading—is that the human heart?

Van Leeuwenhoek: 1675

All day, the cooper's hoops squeal and nibble.
Through the single eyepiece of his hand-ground lens,
he watches a spider's spinnerets, then the tail-strokes
of spermatozoa. Now and then, his bald eye unsquints,
skates blindly across his wrist and sleeve —
and makes from his worlds their reversals:
that of the visible and that of the seen . . .

Visible? he is asked, at the market, or the stone tables
by the river. The lip of the cochineal? Starch
on the membranes of rice? But of course —
though a fashioned glass must press and circle,
tap down, tap down, until that which is, is.

Until that which is, breaks to the eye.
It is much like the purslane, he tells them,
that burst from the hoofbeats of horse soldiers:
black seeds long trapped in their casings, until
the galloping cracked them. In the steppes, he says,

or veldt, where nothing in decades had traveled.
Then flowers burst forth from the trauma
of hoof-taps, and left in the wake of the soldiers
a ribbon of roadway as wide as their riding.

Smoke now. The screech of a shrinking hoop.
His thoughts are floral with hearth flames and soldiers,
the cords in his bent neck rigid as willow.
Then slowly, below, something yellow begins. Some flutter of
yellow on the glass plate, in the chamber of a tubal heart . . .

...

By winter, the snows crossed over the flanks
of the horses, felling them slowly. And the soldiers,
retreating, so close to survival, crept
into the flaccid bellies. Two nights,
or three, hillocks of entrails steaming like
breath. Now and then they called out
to each other, their spines at the spines
of the long horses, and the flaps of muscle
thick shawls around them. Then they rose, as a thaw
cut a path to the living.

. . . A flutter, yellow, where an insect heart ripples
in reflex. But no, it is only light and shadow, light
turning shadow. As the perfect doors, in their terrible
finitude, open and open.

He straightens, feels his body swell
to the known room. Such vertical journeys, he thinks,
down, then back through the magnifications
of light. And the soldiers, their cloaks
like blossoms on a backdrop of snow:
surely, having taken through those hours
both the cradle and the grave,
they could enter any arms and sleep.

Six in All

Three

That we could block these warring worlds — the native
from the fashioned — would make my mother flinch,
although she dips against the larch with languid
resolution, Jane in fever at her feet, my father
with his pipe bowl lifted, pinched,
as he might gently pinch
some brier sparrow into flight . . . that
on this greenhouse wall our faded wisps of family,
reduced to amber filaments, could keep
the cool and hot apart . . .

At times when stark daylight recedes, my present face,
in pale reflection, bobs
near its childhood other — while under the dappled
layers of us, the slack-jawed orchids steam.

Two worlds. Or one, perhaps. Two rival
atmospheres. Once my father crept beneath the sea,
along some vein of miner's shaft. He told
how shaft heat sucked and swelled,
how pallid torsos of the men

gleamed like pulpit lilies. The icy sea so close above
a pin might bring it down, he said.
Two dozen fathoms rushing by. Just overhead,
he heard the boulders shift and roll,
like great-boots pacing on his grave.

■■■

He tossed the brier bird—launched it into flame,
at least—then stepped into the war. Can you believe,
he wrote to us, a field of corn for camouflage?
The frightened soldiers, just stalks themselves
in cultivated blue, dipped and hid, or so they thought—
their crouching image everywhere, like evening
through some giant harp. The corncobs burst
and rained about them, the brindled, bullet-blasted
leaves. On one dead man, the kernels' milk
had glued thick corn-silk to his throat.
It swayed a bit in the August breeze, from
breastbone toward his shoulderline.
As I have seen some bloodless moss
sway from hothouse trees.

Shawl: Dorothy Wordsworth at Eighty

Any strong emotion tempers my madnesses.
The death of beloveds. William in his fever-coat.
I reenter the world through a shallow door
and linger within it, conversations returning,
the lateral cycle of days.

I do not know what it is that removes me,
or sets me again at our long table, two crescents
of pike on a dark plate. But memory lives then,
and clarity. Near my back once again,
our room with a brook at the baseworks,
its stasis of butter and cheese. Or there,

in a corner, my shawl of wayside flowers.
Orchis and chicory. Little tongues of birth-wort.

I remember a cluster of autumn pike
and a dark angler on the slope of the weir.
The fish in his hand and the roiling water
brought forth with their brightness
his leggings and waist. But his torso was lost
into shadow, and only his pipe smoke survived,
lifting, then doubling, on the placid water above him.

Often, I think, I encompass a similar shadow.

But rise through it, as our looped initials
once rose over dye-stained eggs.
We were children. With the milk of a burning candle
we stroked our letters to the hollowed shells.
And dipped them, then, in a blackberry bath,

until the script of us surfaced,
pale, independent, the *D* and cantering *W*.

Then *C* for Christopher. *V*—William laughed—for vale.
And *P*, he said, for Pisces, Polaris, the gimballing
planets. And for plenitude, perhaps,
each season, each voice in its furrow of air . . .

Once, I was told of a sharp-shinned hawk
who pursued the reflection of its fleeing prey
through three striations of greenhouse glass:
the arrow of its body cracking first into anteroom,
then desert, then the thick mist
of the fuchsias. It lay in a bloodshawl
of ruby flowers, while the petals of glass
on the brick-work floor repeated its image.
Again and again and again.
As all we have passed through sustains us.

The Suicide of Clover Adams: 1885

All the bodies like fallen cattle.
And the snub-brimmed caps. The war. Civil.
Brady's shadow, at times, rinses a photograph
with its black pond. But the image I keep

is a blasted meadow. Burdock, bloated sacs
of lungwort. And up from the earth's fresh trough,
I think, the mineral scent of ripped grasses.

Henry slumps in the grip of a toothache.

If I were real, I would help him. But I
am the fabric of well-water—slick and transparent—
my voice a bird where my shoulder should be.

In the Doctrine of Signatures, each plant
cures the body it mimics.
So the liver-shaped leaves of hepatica
temper the liver's jaundice, and snuff
from the snapdragon's tapered neckline
heals the tubular body of the human throat.

Heart leaf and toothwort.

Steam from the kettle
has cast a late dew on the ladles.
And a privacy to each of the windows.
In print after print, Brady centered the men
facing east. The sandbags and cannons.
One midday, I centered our cousins with an eastward
glance, fresh for the incoming hour.

In the darkroom musk, they
rose through potassium baths
with the languorous ripples of flounders . . .

Steam. Its simmering mist.
If I were real, I would offer a flower. But I

have taken a body of water, stirred
through with cyanide salts. Slick and transparent,
they stroke their signature to the echoing self.
Which is nothing. And from which
nothing rises at all.

Vespertilio

—Julia Margaret Cameron

Like winter fog, the coal dust climbs her stockings,
although the coal itself has long departed, tumbled
barrow by barrow to an alternate shelter.
She scrubs the floor, sets across the gaping boards
square vats of rank collodion, of alcohol
and pyrogallol. Still the coal dust blooms,
until her apron darkens and her hem-strokes
brush to the path's pale stones

a soft hieroglyphics. She has walked
to the glass henhouse and bundles the hens
to their new roost, one wing at her breast, one wing
in her hand, the stiff legs riding her forearm.
Their livingness, she says, touching
a wattle and ruby comb, the tepid feet that stretch,
then curl, like something from the sea.

So the coalshed becomes her darkroom
and the henhouse welcomes the bent Carlyle,
Darwin and Tennyson, Browning, Longfellow,
each posed near a curtained backdrop, each

sharp in his livingness: a glaze of amber earwax,
a leaf of tobacco like ash on the beard.
But the portraits . . . Unfocused, critics say. The lens
stepping down into fog. Aberrant. Distorted. Although
she prefers Undefined, as in Not yet captured

...

by the language of this world. They are rich
with the inner, she answers, with a glimpse of the soul
flapping up through collodion baths,

darkly transparent, like the great bats
that flap near the henhouse windows. She watches them
break at dusk past the tree line
then flash at the windows and flash, as if
they are seeking their lost counterparts—although
they are not birds, of course, but dense with wings,
so dense the sleek, half-opened wings

would cover a wattle, a comb, and opening, easily
cover the back, the breast,
and easily opening cover the tail,
the yellow, tepid, stretching feet: like
a dark sea spreads over its garden.

Six in All

Four

*The pulpit lilies gaped and dipped. The coffin's velvet
cast its nap in variative strips, as wind
might cast a summer's wheat. Asleep, they said,
she looks asleep — if sleep can suck the cheek skin down,
can still the lids to bone. I think*

*she had six words in all. And so she thought
in reds and whites, in hard-spun
roundnesses. One afternoon,
my father pressed her fingers to his pipe, breathed in,
exhaled, breathed in, that she might feel, like
some enchanted heart, the pipe bowl flare and ebb.
From that time on, she tracked its brier flutterings,*

*and all the spheres about her: the rigid arc
of radishes, the nurse's knees
that rose and sank beneath her white-knit stockings
like tandem bellies of dying fish.*

*On the pane beside my sister's face,
the glass-plate negative reveals a soldier
dead for weeks, or starved before his death,
his belly just a sunken sling between the bracket
of his hips. Above it all his stiffened belt
orbits like a jester's hoop. The hoop and then a gap
of air, and then the bones of him. And*

*to the right, in sawgrass and a twining vetch,
his cup and round canteen.*

"Death's thimbles," Father called the cups,
the way they steered to softer cloth
a bullet's leaded point. Invisibly the soldiers ran,
until the moonlight caught the cups, until
each pockmarked curve of tin
flared its dimpled bull's-eye.

And so we die of glimmer after all.

Jane's nurse was kind, but by her presence
verified the death at hand. We longed each night
to watch her lift her cape, drape its hood across
her hair, step into the field. The night absorbed her
instantly, the open, blue-black flapping cape
no more than tree limb, shrubbery. Departing,
she was just the world, the way the world
recedes at night. Then at the ridge
she turned to wave
and flashed her ghastly whiteness back at us.

Edison: 1910

Dressed in an ebony suit,
could the soul of William James, they asked me, slip
past the bakery counter, his slack lapels
dusty with flour? Or walk on the cobbles
in those soft shoes? It was God, of course,
not James they questioned. And No, I said, No
suit, no Deity. We are the finite, meat-mechanisms

of matter. The uproar then! He was seen—dark shoes,
trousers—all the newsprint dripping with sightings!
Look down to your own shoes, I told them. There,
in the fluoroscope's green wash, your Inmost Essence

flexes. I remember Dally in his white coat,
week after week, bent
to the X-ray's beam, to the bloat
of ghostly photos, as the peephole burned its round tattoo
on his brow and cheekbone. How the beam itself
nibbled him—fingers, toes, hair, spleen.

A lantern through dust, he whispered, is a kind of gill.
It was Wednesday, a week from his death, some
childhood dust storm storming again.
He spoke of its wind and the launched soil,
the anemone-sway of the darkened sheep, as slowly,
heads dropped, they crossed, recrossed
the smallest arc of battered turf.
And lamplight in the barn,

although it was midday. And although it was midday
the sunset began. Crimson, he said,

just over the sheep, just over the alders, the yellow
sweep of hedgerow. And false, of course, some light
at play on the facets of dust. But . . . wonderful,

he told me. His bones on the fluoroscope's pale screen
tapered and flared, the nodules of toe-tips
black, protrusive, like ghastly buds—a presence

that walks with us always, I think, flexing its grip
invisibly. And that visible sunset he fashioned,
slumped on its false horizon?
Some vibrant, wind-churned absence,
defined by dust and reverence.

Muybridge

These are the names of the horses:
Occident. Elaine. Abe Edgerton. Clay.
With a shutter's quick clickings, I stopped them,
then dealt the divine and its opposite, picture
by square picture: the unwinged body in flight—
two hooves pushing off, then one, then none—
and the pact of that flight: groping forelegs,
the horn-sheathed toes thrust out like cane tips.

Time after time, from the beauty of motion
came the pickets of stasis! And yet,

I remember the heart of a snapping turtle,
grotesque in its florid two-step. We had peeled back
the breastplate, dragged the body by cart past the eyes
of twelve cameras, the cart wheels tripping the shutters.
I could not watch the motion then, but
turned instead to the open mouth, the palate ridged
like a walnut shell, turned instead to the static photos—
where something, hollow and weightless, a poppy perhaps,
where something twelve times, like a poppy,
was pressed and released by a rhythmic wind.

I stopped the pine snake and horse. Or better,
I held them. Field cat. Hawk. The wake
of a coastline steamer.

In a northwest harbor one autumn, I watched a meadow
flood to a cranberry pond. Then a man with a rake
pulled the blunt berries from their soft vines.
They floated around him, filling the surface,

red and amber and that last yellow before it is red.
He stood in the pond, and the berries, like evening,
absorbed him, his boots and thighs. They covered each
glisten of the water, until only the sharpest shining
survived, where the rake cut a path through the redness.

What would I hold? All. Almost all. The poppy
in its soft backdrop. The hawk. And the horse,
the great weight on the last hoof,
then the lifting of that weight.
What would I stop? Only the path
of the rake, I think, that arc
reaching over the pond and the circling hour.
Only the need to reach over.

Six in All

Five

Along the foreground's dusty scrub, a cello's ice-white shadow
slinked toward my mother's hem. Beyond the frame,
the army band was mute across the ground: one flute,
then thwirrs of shuffling cards, like pigeon wings.

And to the left the birds themselves,
the homing cotes and landing boards.

My parents posed against an oak, Jane's carriage thick
beside them—no Jane at all, except for fists
that groped above the basket rim like pearly mums.
My mother smiled, leaned back across my father's arm.
A soldier coughed. No war in sight, no long descent
from dampened bone, to human grain, to
just some frontal profile in the earth. And so,

when from the trees the little shape began,
arced toward us like some triggered stone, we held
our leisure. The bird stoked down, the burl of message
on its leg just words—although I think their secret
finished us. In time, hawk-ripped or ripped by shot,

still the pigeons stuttered back. I wondered
at their steadfastness. The jerking head, the shad-roe eye—
they seemed to crack through clouds
like energy and nothing more. Not drawn by words, of course,
but . . . what? The mate? The suet bead? The humid cote
or human hand? The chime of some vestigial song?
I cannot find the words for this. I think

...
*of oaks, a shutter's gape, the field drums
curved like calves across the ground.*

Burning the Fields

1.

In the windless late sunlight of August,
my father set fire to a globe of twine. At his back,
the harvested acres of bluegrass and timothy
rippled. I watched from a shallow hill
as the globe, chained to the flank of his pickup truck,
galloped and bucked down a yellow row, arced
at the fire trench, circled back,
arced again, the flames behind
sketching first a C, then closing to O—a word
or wreath, a flapping, slack-based heart,

gradually filling. To me at least. To the mare
beside me, my father dragged a gleaming fence,
some cinch-corral she might have known,
the way the walls moved rhythmically,
in and in. And to the crows, manic
on the thermals? A crescent of their planet,

gone to sudden sun. I watched one stutter
past the fence line, then settle
on a Hereford's tufted nape,
as if to peck some safer grain, as if
the red-cast back it rode
contained no transformations.

2.

A seepage, then, from the fire's edge: there
and there, the russet flood of rabbits.

Over the sounds of burning, their haunted calls
began, shrill and wavering, as if
their dormant voice strings
had tightened into threads of glass.

In an instant they were gone—the rabbits,
their voices—over the fire trench,
into the fallows. My father walked
near the burn line, waved up to me, and from
that wave, or the rippled film of heat,

I remembered our porch in an August wind,
how he stepped through the weathered doorway,
his hand outstretched with some
book-pressed flower, orchid or lily, withered
to a parchment brown. *Here,* he said, but
as he spoke it atomized before us—
pulp and stem, the pollened tongue,
dreadful in the dancing air.

3.

Scummed and boxcar thin,
six glass-walled houses stretched beside our fields.
Inside them, lilies, lilies—

a thousand shades of white, I think.
Eggshell, oyster, parchment, flax.

Far down the black-mulched beds, they seemed
ancestral to me, the fluted heads of
dowagers, their meaty, groping,
silent tongues. They seemed

to form perspective's chain:
cinder, bone, divinity . . .

4.

My father waved. The crows set down.
By evening, our fields took the texture
of freshened clay, a sleek
and water-bloated sheen, although no water
rested there—just heat and ash
united in a slick mirage. I crossed the fence line,
circled closer, the grasses all around me
collapsing into tufts of smoke. Then as I bent
I saw the shapes, rows and rows of tougher stems—

brittle, black, metallic wisps, like something grown
to echo grass. The soot was warm,
the sky held smoke in a jaundiced wing,
and as a breeze crossed slowly through,
stems glowed—then ebbed—
consecutively. And so revealed a kind of path,
and then a kind of journey.

Depth of Field

Specula. Gauze in a halo of disinfectant.
We sit in the small room, dimmed
by the X-ray of my father's chest
and the screen's anemic light. Because on film
the spots are dark, my mother asks
if, in the lung, they might be white: some
hopeless sense of the benign. My father smiles.
Outside the window, a winter storm
continues. Across the park, the bronze-cast generals
spur their anguished horses, each posture
fierce with rearing. Nostrils, lips, the lidless eyes.
Now all the flung-back heads have filled with snow.

After-Image

Three weeks past my father's death
his surgeons, in pond-green smocks, linger,
trail after me from dream to porch, down
the bark and needle pathway toward the river.
One nudges me, explains, as he did weeks ago,
the eye's propensity for opposites, why green
displaced their bleached-white coats. Looking up
from the tablet of a patient's blood, he says,
the red-filled retina will cast a green
on every white it crosses. A phantom wash
on a neighboring sleeve. It startles us,
he tells me. And: Green absorbs the ghosting.
                    Then he is gone, the path
returning to boot brush and the squirrel ratchets
my father loved. It is noon, the sky
through the tree limbs a sunless white.
I have come to watch the spawning salmon
stalled in the shallow pools. Age
has burned them a smoky red, though
their heads are silver, like helmets. Just over
the mossy floor, they float unsupported,
or supported by the air their gills have winnowed.
I think I will gather them soon, deep
in the eye, red and red and red,
then turn to the canopy of sky and cedars.
It will support them soon, the green.

Six in All

Six

Behind my back, before my family, the elms
have flared, dropped leaves, regathered them in tiny buds.
Before me, behind my family, the limes are still,
drawn out through shades of darkening
by nothing more than light. Last night

I read a tracker's lore, half truth, I think,
half wonderment—how, fleeing, one man mounted stilts,
another fastened to his soles the stiffened gnarls
of cows' hooves. Such fussings over twists
in dust! But beauty, too, that one can read
a residue, that from the profile of a stride
a body might be crafted.

We're faded now, my mother's sleeve, my sister's spidered
fists. For someone standing next to me,
we're only hatchings on the glass, like

hairline prints the heron leaves,
its tracks across the sandy bank first shallow—here—
then deeper as a fish was snared, then deeper still
as, taking flight, it most was wedded to the ground.

But I've described a positive, the darkened prints
across the glass. In fact these hatch-lined negatives
echo what was pale in us. And if the bird had truly walked
in tandem with my family's path, its tracks
would yield a vacancy, like whitened lashes
of the dead. In this inert, inverted world,

what most engaged the passing light tumbled first
to nothingness. My father lifts a brier pipe,
a soot-black bulb reversed to ice.
The stem, the bowl, the mouthpiece gone.
It is his smoke that lingers.

FROM *The Seconds* (2001)

The Seconds

—Claude Laurent, glassblower, 1850

With a flurry of sidestrokes, the March wind
swims down the chimney, its air chafed
by hearth smoke and bacon. It is sunset,

and high on the inglenook shelf,
a gauze of crystal flutes
captures the lamplight. I am their maker—Laurent—
eased back in a soft chair, listening

to hearth logs sag through the andirons.
And thinking of seconds—first time, of course, then
the hapless devoted who step from behind
with their handkerchiefs and swords, ready to give shape
to another's passion, as a body gives shape to a soul.

When the handkerchief crosses the damp grass,
they must wish it all back, the seconds:
that the handkerchief rise,
flap back to the hand, and the passion
pull back to its source, as the sword and the pistol
pull back to their sheaths.
Then everything silent, drawn in by some vast,
improbable vacuum—
as an orchestra of ear trumpets might silence a room!

Now the wall clock taps. Across my knees
the house cat casts her rhythmic thrum.
Once I lifted a flute, some second

blemished by a loll in the lime, and blew
through its crystal body a column of pipe smoke.
I remember its hover just over my chest,
a feral cloud
drawn down and bordered, it seemed
in that evening light, not by glass
but by itself.

Seconds and smoke . . .
Into what shape will our shapelessness flow?

Outside my window,
two children bob in the late light,
walking with their mother on the furrowed fields.
They love how their shadows
are sliced by the troughs—how, over the turned rows,

their darkened, elongated shapes
rush just ahead in segments, waving
their fractured sleeves. Now their mother
is laughing, lifting her arms and pale boot,
watching her sliced and rippled
shadow—whose parallel is earth, not she,
whose shape is taken not by her, but the cyclic light

her shape displaces. Now her head,
now her shoulder,
now the drop of her long coat

have stretched to some infinite black bay
pierced by the strokes of a black swan.

"Will You Walk in the Fields with Me?"

—Early dueling challenge

They are matted with frost
and a porous cloth that is the season's first snow.
The fields. The seconds.

And the firsts, of course, their manored lords.

Seen from above in the dawn light, the burgundy,
snow-dappled cloaks of the lords
are two cardinal points of a compass,
its jittery needle defined
by the segmented footprints of sixteen paces.

It is the moment after turning. No one has fallen,
one bullet passing through a hat brim, the other
entering a birch tree with the sound
of a hoof through shallow ice.

At their fixed points, the lords wait. Winter wind
sails through their cloaks. They have entered the dawn
carrying no more than a *sense of self*, the magnetic pull
of decorum, and stand now, smiling a little,
satisfaction obtained by a hat brim,

by a birch that shivers in the early light, as

the seconds do, stomping in place in the snow.
They have entered the dawn carrying, in fact,
two bladders of salve, tourniquets browned

by an aging sun. No selves at all, they
are empty, waiting to be called, waiting to step forth
in another's image—the hat plume and cloak,

after his likeness, the footfalls and trembling. Waiting,
with his grace, to make their turn,

while deep in the dawn's new day, a little
circle of darkness draws a heart-high bead
and the beasts of the fields stand steaming.

The Last Castrato

—1904

Buoyed by light, the gaping, bronze recording horn
floats near his upturned face, near his lips
that echo in their opaque sheen
the wax now turning at the horn's slim tip.
He is offering Hasse's aria—pale suns in the misty heavens,
the tremblings, the hearts. But the stylus slips
on the low notes and fricatives until only
something like *emblem* remains, a *pale, une'en art*
etching the cylinder's tranquil curl. And so

he is asked to compromise: the lowered tongue, the softened
voice, a forfeiture for permanence. But compromise
has brought him here. And softening. And permanence
has poured its liquid bronze into the gap
the temporary held so steadfastly. He steps away, steps
back. What on earth to do? Encircle loss, finite
and full-throated, as the stylus drops his highs and lows,
his suns and heavens, his seamless climbs from heart to mist?
Or forfeit loss and, so, be saved?

Testament: Vermeer in December

To my daughter, Elsbeth, two loaf-sized, secret coffers.
To my sons, the pastel seascape.
And the peat chest. And the Spanish chairs, perhaps.
And the ivory-capped cane at rest on my bedstead.
And the sheets, and the ear cushions,

and the seventeen pocket handkerchiefs
that flap at the summons of each dawn's catarrh.
Now and then, through their linen expanse
I revisit my children, in flight down an iced stream,
their sail-pushed sleds clicking, clicking
like a covey of walnut carts. . . .

To my servant, *Bass Viol with Skull.*
The wicker cradle. The ash-gray travel mantle.
To the men who will carry my coffin,
glass flasks — six — and a marbled flute

carved from the wing bone of a mute swan.
Its music may offer a tremoloed solace
as they lift from the gravesite my infant son.
Two years in the earth, his wooden box, darkened
by marl and a bleeding silt, will ride
my greater other like a black topknot
as we are lowered in tandem down the candlelit walls.

To my wife, the yellow jacket, silk and fur-trimmed,
that warms, through the mirror of a linseed wash,
a hazel-haired woman eternally lit by a pearl necklace.
She carries, with a dabble of madder and burnt ocher,
the wistful, enigmatic gaze of my children

...

as they circled the pale flute, dreaming they said of some
haunted voice, deep in a gliding wing, its song
both shrill and melodic,
like the cry of an infant controlled by a choir.

And to you, in half-rings around me, your faces
spaced like pearls . . . imagine that moment
when the ropes are lowered and something begins
on the lit walls, shape over shape: I leave it to you,
that shadowed conjunction of matter and light
that flies, in its fashion, between us.

The Magic Mountain

To sit on a balcony, fattened by lap robes and a fur pouch,
with the columbines nodding in their earthen pots
and the weighted autumn moon
already casting to the balustrade

a rim of tepid frost, is to know to the bones
the crepuscular slumber of bats—
alit between seasons of dawn and day, day and dusk,
and everything turning, perpetually. . . .

This evening's soup was studded with cloves—
brown pods and corollas—the diminutive heads of
    sunflowers.
To my left, in a neighboring balcony window,
a young man is dying, face turned to the ceiling,
his red chin beard sparse and pointed. He is joined
by a woman with a parchment fan, although I see only

her hand and cuff, the curve of a damask sleeve.
And a sky of rootless willows, gray, yellow-green,
pleated in parchment, swaying a little as the hand sways,
folding at last to a single stem. And then a sleight

of magic comes: from the fan's handle
a face is formed, spar by closing spar.
Egyptian, I think. The hooded eyes. The slender beard.
Each spar tucks down to its thin contribution,
earlobe or cheekbone, a slice of brow—
and there! one full-blown, ivory face, perfect
on her damask knees.

...

Now the bats are aloft, stroking in pairs past the pallid moon.
Once, in the twilit dust of the X-ray room,
I saw on the screen a human lung,
abundant and veined as a willow.

In his bed the young man is stirring, and the woman
has lifted her parchment fan, the ivory face
shining a moment in the facets of lamplight

before its surrender to gray, yellow-green.
And which is the better, I wonder:
To gather from parts such a fullness?
Or to part into fullness so breathtakingly?

Pasteur on the Rue Vauquelin

Near the red blade of a furred poinsettia,
just to the left of the stamen cluster, a dragonfly slowly
dips and lifts. In the grasp of its tendril legs
floats a yellow almond, or a child's thimble perhaps, or
some bulbous facet of light. It is dawn. The boy,
Joseph Meister, is sleeping, his necklace

of cauterized dog bites
glowing like topaz. In delirium,
he mumbles of scarves and ale tents, how a jester
thumbs back a tankard's lid, and then—
the snarl of a weasel in a woven cap.

This is the grand hour, light coming toward me
in fragments, as if to prepare me
for its greater flood. . . .

When I was a boy, floods toppled the fence posts
and birches. And once,
I watched at the depth of a shovel's blade
yellow turnips afloat in a tepid sea. Their rocking
sent sets of concentric rings,
and there—three Saturns just under my feet!

Dawn. From my soft chair I am tempering rabies
with injections of . . . *rabies!* And tracking
the path of a yellow light, flower to memory to
a mirror of sky. How it dips and lifts
with its quick sting, synapse to synapse.
How that which invades us, sustains us.

The Highland

—Zelda Fitzgerald, 1939

Dear One,

Do you have the time? Can you take
the time? Can you make
the time?

To visit me? The hospital doors have opened to spring,
and its land *is* high, dear one, each slope
with a vapor of crocuses. Its citizens, alas,

are low. Despondent, in fact, though a jar of sun tea
tans on the sill. The woman beside me
has opened the gift of a china doll, an antique
Frozen Charlotte. Glass face, a cap of china hair,
shellacked to the sheen of a chestnut.

At breakfast the shifting returned, dreadful
within me: *colors were infinite, part of the air . . .*
lines were free of the masses they held. The melon,
a cloud; and the melon, an empty,
oval lariat.

They have moved the canvas chair
from the window. Sun, enhanced
by the brewing jar, threw
an apricot scorch on the fabric. The fruit,
a cloud. The fruit,
a doll-sized, empty lariat.

...

D. O., into what shape
will our shapelessness flow?

Dear One,

Italian escapes me. Still, I float to the operas
of Hasse and Handel, a word now and then
lifting through . . . *sole, libertà*. In an earlier time,
the thrum-plumped voice of a countertenor—half male,
half female—might place him
among us, we who are thickened
by fracturings. D. O., now and then, my words

break free of the masses they hold.
Think of wind, how it barks through the reeds
of a dog's throat. How the pungent, meaty stream of it
cracks into something like words—but not. I just sit

in the sun room then, slumped in my fur and slabber,
feeling the wolf begin, back away, then some
great-jawed, prehistoric other
begin, back away, then the gill-less,
the gilled, then the first pulsed flecks
begin, back away, until only a wind remains,
vast and seamless. No earth, no heavens.
No rise, no dip. No single flash of syllable
that might be me. Or you.

D. O.,

Now a gauze of snow on the crocuses! I woke
to its first brilliance—midnight, great moon—
and walked through the hallways. The pin-shaped leaves
of the potted cosmos threw a netted shadow,

and I stopped in its fragile harmony,
my arms, bare feet, the folds of my limp gown
striped by such weightless symmetry
I might have been
myself again. Through an open screen door

I saw a patient, drawn out by the brightness perhaps,
her naked body a ghastly white, her face
a ghastly, frozen white, fixed
in a bow-mouthed syncope, like something

out of time. As we are, D. O., here
in the Highland, time's infinite, cyclic now-and-then
one simple flake of consciousness
against the heated tongue.

_____

Dear One,

My Italian improves:
sole, libertà,
and *Dio,* of course, D. O.! (Although He
has forsaken me.) The tea at the window
gleams like the flank of a chestnut horse. It darkens

imperceptibly, as madness does, or dusk.
All morning, I held a length of cotton twine—
a shaggy, oakum filament—
between the jar and brewing sun.
We made a budding universe: the solar disc,

the glassy globe of reddish sea, the stillness
in the firmament. At last across the cotton twine
a smoke began, a little ashless burn, Dio,

that flared and died so suddenly
its light has yet to reach me.

Concentration

We understand the egg-sized ship,
the thread-and-spindle masts, the parchment sails
puffed to a rigid billow.

And the lightbulb that enfolds it.

We understand the man, Graham Leach, his passion for
impossibles. We see him,
tucked within the vapor of his jasmine tea,

while heron-toed forceps slowly wed

a deckhand to a tear of glue.
The rudder would lodge in the bulb's slim throat
but could be folded, slipped inside, reopened

into seamlessness. We understand that sleight of hand

but not this full-sized pocket watch
upright in a 30-watt. Perhaps it's made of lesser stuff
than gold, some nonmetallic pliancy. Still,

it mirrors the museum shelf, and to the left

the plump barque, static in its perfect globe.
Perhaps he blew a gaping bulb
then tucked the watch inside, rewarmed the glass,

drew out a path, clamped one end's concentric rings,
■■■

the contact point's dark star. This would explain
what we've attributed to time
and now must give to fire: the amber face,

the wrinkled Roman numerals—

still fixed, still spaced to mark the intervals
of space, but rippled,
a dozen, ashless filaments. The filament

itself is gone. Gold's light enough, perhaps.

We understand, to make a living bulb,
three hundred wicks were tried. Before a match was found.
Oakum, fishline, flax, plumbago. A coconut's

starched hair. A sprig of human beard.

Three hundred tries, before some agent, tucked
within a vacuum globe, could catch the rasp
outside—that friction-fed, pervasive tick—

and channel it, and draw it in.

Orbit

For warmth in that Swedish winter, the child,
aged one, wore petticoats hooked from angora,
knotted and looped to a star-shaped weave.
And for her father, there at the well lip,
she did seem to float in the first magnitude—
alive and upright, far down the cylindric dark,
with the star of her petticoats
buoyantly rayed on the black water.
One foot in the water bucket, one foot
glissading a brickwork of algae, he stair-stepped
down, calling a bit to her ceaseless cries, while
his weight, for neighbors working the tandem crank,
appeared, disappeared, like a pulse.
In bottom silt, the mottled snails
pulled back in their casings
as her brown-shoed legs lifted, the image
for them ancient, limed with departure:
just a shimmer of tentacles
as the skirt of a mantle collapsed
and a shape thrust off toward answering shapes,
there, and then not, above.

Latitude

With a framework of charts and reckonings, reason tells us

they died from time, the rhythmic tick of hub and blade
that, turning, turned their fuel to mist.

And reason says, while Earhart held the plane

balanced as a juggler's plate, Noonan tipped the octant
toward the stars, and then, no radios
to guide them, toward the dawn and rising sun.

On the hot, New Guinea runway, they'd lifted glasses,
a scorch of mango juice brilliant in their hands.
Around their heels, a dog-sized palm leaf fretted,
then the cockpit's humid air slowly chilled to atmosphere
and there was nothing: two thousand miles
of open sea, theory, friction, velocity. The weighted *ifs*,

the hair-thin, calibrated *whens*. Reason says they died

from time and deviation. That vision can't be trusted:
the octant's sightline, quivered by an eyelash,
the compass needle, vised by dust, sunlight's runway
on the water, even the slack-weave net of longitude

cast to gather time and space, a few salt stars,
the mackerel sky. The folly of its dateline
throws travelers into yesterday, and so the snub-nose plane
quickly crossed into the past, and stalled, and sank,

the theories say, one hour *before* departure.

...

Reason asks for grace with time, a little latitude
that lets a dateline shiver at the intervals of loss
and gain. As vision does, within
those intervals—and though it can't be trusted, still
it circles back, time and time again:

the black Pacific closing over them. And then,
the click of glasses, orange and radiant.

Grand Forks: 1997

An arc of pips across a playboard's field
tightens, then, in the Chinese game of Go,
curls back to weave a noose, a circle closing, closed.

Surrounded, one surrenders. Blindsided,
collared from behind. Then silence, or so
my friends revealed, the arc across their patchwork fields

not pips, but flood. The dikes collapsed, they said;
the river, daily, swelled. Then *pastures* rose,
as earth's dark water table—brimful—spilled, and closed

behind their backs, the chaff-filled water red
with silt, with coulees, creeks, a russet snow,
all merging from behind. Then through the bay-bright fields

a dorsal silence came. And, turning, filled
the sunken streets, the fallen dikes, the slow,
ice-gripped periphery where frozen cattle closed

across their frozen likenesses. Mirrored,
as when the Northern Lights began, their glow
was mirrored, green to green, across the flooded fields—
like haunted arcs of spring, one circle closing, closed.

The Circus Riders

—*Marc Chagall, 1969*

Sly-eyed and weightless, my violet rooster
quietly crosses a tent's blue dome.
He is buoyant, inverted, a migrating, wattled chandelier

that blinks from a ceiling's cool expanse
as the astronauts do—now one, now two, now three—
in orbit past a camera lens. While I dapple his beak
with a palette knife—and the acrobat's tights,
and the gallery's blue curve—the astronauts

crackle from space, their silver suits
shining like herring brine. They tell me the stars,
ungrated by atmosphere, do not twinkle at all, but
glow in their slow orbs, like shells on a black beach.
Now and then, through a tiny, waste-water door,

a galaxy of urine rolls, each oval drop bloated,
indistinguishable, they say, from the stars.
And the sextant quivers through this human heaven!

On a sky of henna and cypress green,
a purple moon lingers. I placed to its left
a grandfather clock, massive, floating up
from a village's peaked roofs, then tilting to gravity's arc.
With its walls and weightless precision, my clock

...

seems a spacecraft's twin, a few seconds—
lacquered to history—pressed to the crystal
like faces. When I was ten, the Russian woods held a haze
of white birches. Specters, I thought, that sidestroked
at night past my open window, their leafy hoods
rattling. And now they are back,

waving from space, humming Dvořák's minor keys—
the plaintive A's, the pensive E's—their world
a little bead of sound
in that vast, unbroken soundlessness. A little
glint, and rhythmic tick.

⸻

No chemist, Delacroix!
His paints will not dry.
Over time, the horse heads would sag into roan melons,
the portraits scowl, the lions relax their clenched jaws,

were they not, on alternate years, hung upside down
on their brass hooks—walls of inverted Delacroixs
regaining their borders, seeping back into neck scarves
and bridles, as my specters seeped back into
birch leaves. On those lessening nights, I watched

my father, asleep in his slim bed. His shoulders
and chest. Now and then, the glisten of herring scales
at his wrists. Head back, his full beard pointed toward
Mars, he seemed balanced there between death
and exertion, while the tannery's smells—sharp
as the odors of art—swept over us, and its
paddocked cattle, in the frail balance
of their own hours, shifted and lowed.

...

So this was the body
emptied. Exhausted. I stood between
terror and splendor as time and what must be
the soul—as the day and the day's morning—
seeped back to him.

And so they are circling back, the riders,
a talc of pumice on their boot soles.
When it all began, they said, and gravity
first dropped its grip, an effluvium of parts
flew up, hidden from brooms and the vacuum:

a curl of ash, a comb's black tooth, one slender
strip of cellophane, and what must have stung
those steady hearts: a single, silver screw—

now vertical, now cocked, now looping slowly
past each troubled face. . . . But nothing failed,
and so they've turned, the fire of their engines

a violet-feathered plume. My acrobat kicks up
one weightless leg. And holds. Across the room
a green tea brews. Their pulses
must have lurched, then stalled—the screw, the soft,
undissipated curl of ash: their craft
was crafted, and, crafted, flawed!

I see them in their silver suits, stunned
to numbness, as, looping slowly by, two sets
of pale, concentric rings fused nothing
more than air and human quickening.

...

An eye-blink's time, perhaps, before they felt
themselves return: that wash of rhythmic strokes,
that hum.

But that was their
moment, their wonder.

I tremble before my own heart.

FROM *First Hand* (2005)

Prologue

They darken. In the sky over Florence,
the oblong clouds swell and darken.
And hailstones lift back through the updrafts,
thickening, darkening, until, swollen as bird eggs,
they drop to the cobbled streets.

Horses! the child Galileo thinks, then
peeks through the doorway
to the shock of ten thousand icy hooves.
At his back, his father is tuning violins,
and because there is nothing sharper at hand

Galileo saws through a captured hailstone
with a length of E-string,
the white globe opening slowly, and the pattern inside
already bleeding its frail borders.
Layers and layers of ice —

Like what? Onion pulp? Cypress rings?
If only the room were colder, and the eye
finer. If only the hand were faster,
and the blade sharper, and firmer,
and without a hint of song . . .

Time and Space

Deep space. The oblong, twinkle-less stars
matte as wax pears. And the astronauts are losing heart,
the heady lisp of auricle and ventricle
fading to a whisper, as muscles shrink to infants' hearts,
or the plum-shaped nubs of swans.
Atrophy, from time in space, even as the space in time
contracts. And how much safer it was—
ascension—at some earlier contraction, each flyer intact,

cupped by a room-sized celestial globe
staked to a palace lawn. How much easier, to duck
with the doublets and powdered wigs
through the flap of a trapdoor and watch on a soot-stained
copper sky the painted constellations, or,
dead-center, a fist of shadowed earth dangling from a ribbon.

All systems go, of course: each moist,
diminishing heart, just sufficient at its terminus to fuel
the arm, the opening hand, to coax
to the lips a fig or pleated straw. Still, how much easier
to drift in a hollow globe, its perpetual,
tallow-lit night, while outside with the mazes and spaniels

the day, like an onion, arced up in layers
to the dark heavens. How much safer to enter a time, a space,
when a swan might lift from a palace pond
to cross for an instant—above, below—its outstretched
Cygnus shape, just a membrane
and membrane away. A space in time when such accident
was prophecy, and such singular alignment—
carbon, shadow, membrane, flight—sufficient for the moment.

Counting: Gregor Mendel in the Prelacy

My companions since childhood, these numbers.
My constant counterparts, as lime kilns
steamed on our green hills

and my father grafted to russet knuckles
a golden apple's fingerlings. (That first stalk
six posts from the gate, and the gate
twelve strides from the pond.)

Each winter, I loved the ermine's harmony,
how it stitched over fresh drifts
the parallel pricks of its tracks. And the pale,

symmetrical petals of snow, how they covered
our seventy houses, our eight hundred
yoke of good arable, good meadowland,
our four hundred ninety souls.

Holy Father, do not think that I think of you less
when I think of you mathematically.

Tomorrow, November closes—
and, polished by frost, the church bells
respond with a clarity. Already,

one-fourth of the compost
is eaten by lime, one-third of the belfry
by shadow. How the second hand ticks!
Stay with me, now, as I wind through my first life. . . .

Thinking of Red

—Marie Curie, 1934

Back from the workbench and lamp, the tilt
of the microscope's mantis head, back from the droplet
of sea, salted by powdered radium,
and the lift and swirl of its atoms—the buffed,
invisible globes of its atoms—she sat
with her apple and knife, confined to her wide bed.

I am thinking of red, she said. And those
primary years, gathered like cardinals.
Although there were no cardinals, of course.
But gooseberries. And roe, there was roe
so gold it was red. All the fruit trees were padded
with cabbage leaves, and she climbed, red in her pinafore,

through their crackling branches. Now and then,
from the movements of children above her,
dry cabbage leaves rained a brittle parchment.
And then, just silence, as they sat with their meals
of bread and gooseberries—like mythic birds
in their bright aprons—while the Polish sun,

for miles to the west, cast to their pale,
partitioned land the fractured shadows of fruit trees.
Thinking of red . . . corpuscles, their freight of typhus,
their glowing freight of radium. But—no—today
just the red of those childhood years. Roe.
And apples, how the ships slipped down from Kasmierz,

...

laden with apples. Thin ships, so weighted they seemed
just prow, great horses legging the yellow river.
On deck, she would watch the straw raked back,
as the scent of a thousand russet apples—
nested like cardinals—rose in the winter air.
She could toss to the river the blemished ones—

the captain gave permission—then cover her basket
with perfect others, the red, chilled, perfect
globes, so cold they would fill the season.
But even the blemished lingered awhile,
lifted and dove through the clear air, and sent
to the prows and empty docks, to the winter rafts

and long horizon, their sets of concentric rings.
Before they sank through the closing water,
they lifted and turned as . . . atoms must. Or better,
cardinals. Although there were no cardinals,
of course, just flight and its watery echo, red
over red, over red, as far as the eye could see.

Matins: Gregor Mendel and the Bees

Slowed by smoke, they slump
from the hive,
benign from the hive they slump,
Father of thorax and wing,
Father of light, they light
on my arm, make light
of my arm, tapering, golden,
Father of darkness receding,
they make from my arm
a candle, a flame, they candle
my arm with backcast
light, affixing the self
to the shell.

Prodigy

Lovely, he thinks, stepping off from the shoreline,
how the pond erases his shadow
in equal proportion
to the body its water accepts. Until, as shadow,
he is nothing, just head and an upraised arm —
while, pale in the pond, he is Benjamin Franklin,
a child with a kite on a string.

And now he is cargo, drawn by the wind,
as pond water slaps
and the kite's red gills billow. Such pleasure,
shoulders to toes, all
down the slim, cirrus shape of his body,
to be pulled by the wind, half fish, half bird,

while horse carts clack down the Boston streets, deep
in their own progress, and shadows
slip westward, and the long fingers of tallow,
pale in his father's shop, dip and thicken and dip.

Blue day. On the salt marsh hills, other boys play out
their landlocked strings, crisscrossing
the grasses, heavy as pendulums. Only one,
young Franklin, floats with his kite,

weightless and tethered in equal proportion.
White-knuckled, good-natured, he would wave
if he could. But he is a staple
binding the elements. White knot
at the end of a stitch. And lovely, he thinks, to be

both the knot and the stitch. That
is the secret, isn't it? To be, at once,
all body, all soul. That is the key.

Gregor Mendel in the Garden

Black-robed on the green hillside,
he seems less shape than space—Abbot Napp—
a gap in a flock of April lambs.
Then wind opens his wide sleeves and the flock
scatters—his little ones, his progeny, bred, crossbred.

In this first morning light, I am turning
the garden, kneeling and rising, my apron flapping
its own dark wing. Such a daybreak of drops
and ascensions!—winter on the pebble, sunlight
on the nape, and the black soil swallowing

my pea seeds, like beads through a crow's gullet.
With grace and patience, the Abbot
would cancel in his scattered lambs
the parasites, the strucks and toxin shards
that yearly fell them. But life's eluded him

and so he breeds for beauty: a triple crimp in wool,
a certain glint in lanolin. And the spiral horn—
that curling cornucopia—corrugated, green-cast,
shaped, he says, by repetition's needs.
(*Not unlike your pea pods, Gregor.*)

Beautiful, he tells me, those circling, dusty pleats.
And if only he could breed there some brief
continuation. Another swirl, he says, another turn
on matter's slender axis. Another rise— *Gregor*—
another dip. Before the ripping tip.

Tulips, Some Said

When Abraham Ortelius fell in love with the world,
sometime in the autumn of 1560, and vowed to map
its grand expanse, its seas and serrated coastlines,
that the mind might hold, as it does an onion,
"the weighty, layered wholeness of it,"
a tulip was launched, from Constantinople's limpid port
toward the deep-water docks of Antwerp.
Still tucked in its fleshy bulb, it rode
with a dozen others, rising and falling
near the textile crates, as the ship slowly crossed
the southern sun, past Athens and Napoli, Elba, Marseille.
This is the world, Ortelius said, holding up to his friend,
Pieter Bruegel, a flattened, parchment, two-lobed heart.
And this, Bruegel answered, paint still damp
on his landscape of games, each with its broad-backed child.
It was an autumn of chatter and doubt, wonder
and grief and a quick indignation, sharp as linseed.
Slowly the ship tracked the Spanish coast, rising
and falling as the rains began, and the olives darkened,
and red-tunicked soldiers, increasing their numbers,
rode north toward Flanders. When the bulb
of a tulip is parted—its casing is also a tunic—
it reveals to the eye the whole of itself, all it will need,
like a zygote cell, to enter its own completion:
roots and pulp and, deep at the center,
leaves and a coil of bud.
That is the world, said Pieter. And that, said Abraham,
each beholding the other's expanse: on a single plane,
the oblong, passive hemispheres and, as if caught
by a closer eye, stocky, broad-backed, hive-strewn shapes,
alit in their grave felicity.

Mistaken for an onion, the bulb was roasted
near the Antwerp docks, then eaten with oil and vinegar.
Still new to the region, the others were buried in soil.
In Abraham's early folios, South America blooms
from its western shore, articulating a shape
that has yet to appear, while in Bruegel's dark painting,
a child on a hobbyhorse whips a flank of air.
Neither man lived to see, in 1650, at Nuremberg's
Peace Fair and Jamboree, fifteen hundred boys
on their wooden horses, fifteen hundred beribboned manes.
Watched from the highest balconies, they filled the square
like tulips, some said. Like soldiers, said others.
Although none could be seen completely. At last, all agreed,
they gave to the square a muted, ghostly atmosphere,
like the moods in medieval tapestries
that hold in quiet harmony violence and a trellised rose—
although the sun that day was bright, all agreed,
and the wind splendid and clear, as it carried
the taps of those wooden hooves, and lifted
the ribbons this way and that, this way and that,
until night, like the earth, covered them.

Stroke

To stroke from stone the hovering bee—
to release from marble its white thorax—the hand
must turn back on itself, palm up, fingers curved,
with the gesture of skipping stones over water.
And to sculpt the wings, the hand must arc downward,
fingers stiff, with the gesture of rubbing grief
from the brow. And so, Gianlorenzo Bernini learned,
carving bees for the Pope's family shield, for the churches
and Roman fountains: palm up
in the workshop, palm up in the world; fingers stiff
on the chisel and brow; hand curved to the hammer,
hand curved to the wine glass; palms pressed
for the wafer, palm up for the thorax, the coin,
for the quick rains that washed from his skin
the decades of white dust.

To free Saint Teresa to her ecstasy, or Daphne
to her leafed future, the hand must know first
the promise of wax. Or graphite. Or the tepid flesh
of clay. The hand must know first
the model. These are the angles, Bernini said,
for the animate, human form: acute, obtuse,
salient, re-entering. Hour by passing hour,
his room filled with stone chips and ciphers,
the metallic scent of mathematics. Now and then,
a brief snow tempered his marble horses.
Now and then, migraine headaches made lace
of his world. These are the compasses, slipped
from their soft pouches. And these, the reflex angles
of their pivoting leg, when the hand, circling,
turns back on itself.

···

To curry from stone the texture of silk, or feathers,
or the fluid parchment of bee wings, the hand
must pursue the source, must open to fullness
the brief wing, or the downward slope
of the lover's robe, so that stone might turn back
on itself, might climb through the strata of bedrock
and centuries to echo the living—just as the living
climb down into stone. These are the hand strokes,
Bernini said: frontal, alee, emergent, re-entering.
For the climbing, shapes to their shaped reversals—
as, two days from his death, shapes would climb
through his right arm, through the long wick of his nerves:
little sparks, little Janus flames, lighting their own
departure. Then a thrum, he said. All through the flesh
that thrum. Bees. White bees.

Gregor Mendel and the Calico Caps

With tweezers light as a pigeon's beak,
I have clipped from each stamen a pollen-filled anther:
hour by hour, three hundred tiny beads, dropped
in my robe's deep pocket, their yellow snuff
sealing the seam lines. And thus,

I emasculate peas that would sire themselves.

Heresy, some say,
to peel back the petal, sever the anther, stroke
to the open blossom—with the sweep of a pollen-tipped
paintbrush—another blossom's heritage.
Heresy, to mingle seed

fixed in the swirl of the world's first week.

Rest, now.
The bird-beak tweezers mute on my lap.
In France, where orchards yield to upswept Alps,
they have tied to the legs of pigeons
parchment memoranda—silk threads

encircling the flaccid skin, and a burl of words

that lifts between neighboring rooftops.
Twofold, I believe,
the gift of those gliding wings:
for the mind, script,
for the soul, the sluiced shape of the thermals,

at last made visible to the upturned eye . . .

■■■

My fingers are weary. Snuff in the seam lines.
To ward off the breeze and the bee,
I have tied to each blossom a calico cap. Three hundred
calico caps. From afar in this late-day light,
they nod like parishioners in an open field,

murmuring, stumbling slightly through the green expanse,

as I, in my labors, am stumbling. And all of them
spaced, it appears, on the widening arc
of some grand design. Blossom and cap in some
grand design. Vessel and motion and the tinted threads.
Heresy? Have I not been placed on that widening path?

Am I not, in my calling, among them?

DNA

At hand: the rounded shapes, cloud white, the scissors, sharp,
two dozen toothpick pegs, a vial of amber glue.
It's February, Cambridge, 1953,
and he's at play, James Watson: the cardboard shapes,

two dozen toothpick pegs, a vial of amber glue.
White hexagons, pentagons, peg-pierced at the corners —
he's at play, James Watson, turning cardboard shapes
this way, that. And where is the star-shot elegance

when hexagons, pentagons, peg-pierced at the corners,
slip into their pliant, spiral-flung alignments?
Where is that star-shot elegance? This way? That?
He slips together lines of slender pegs that quickly

split in two. (Pliant, spiral-flung, one line meant
solitude. But one to one? Pristine redundancy.)
He slips. Together, lines of slender pegs quickly
conjugate. White hexagons, white pentagons:

not solitude but — one, two, one — pristine redundancy.
So close the spiral shape, now. Salt and sugar atoms
congregate: white hexagons, white pentagons.
So close the bud, the egg, the laboratory lamb,

the salt and sugar atoms' spiral shape. So close —
it's February, Cambridge, 1953 —
the blossom, egg, the salutary lamb. So close
at hand, the rounded shapes — cloud white — the scissors — sharp.

Questions of Replication:
The Brittle-Star

Why now, under seven fathoms of sea,
with sunlight just a sheen on its carapace
and someone's dark paddle stroking above?
Why, at this moment, does it lift from the reef
its serrated jaws, its four, undulant,
tendril arms—the fifth atomized
by a predator's nudge—to begin
the body's slow unbuckling? Near the reef,
a kick-dust of plankton hovers. And eelgrass.
And far down the sea floor, the true starfish
in their dank, illegible constellations.
What salt-rich analgesic allows
this self-division, as the disc parts
and tendril arms, each with a thousand
calcite eyes, sway into slender helixes?
Half disc and half disc. Limb pair; limb pair.
Two thousand eyes; two thousand crystal eyes—
that must notice now the emergent other,
aslant but familiar, slowly swimming away:
its butterflied, genetic list, its tendency
toward luminescence. Limb over limb,
where is it headed? And when will its absence
echo, adrift in the sea's new weight?
Half shape; half shape—how far will it stroke
before loss, like daylight, lessens,
and the one that remains twines its optic arms
to look to the self for completion?

Redux

They darken. In the ponds and springs near Stuttgart,
the oblong newt eggs swell and darken, cells
and their daughters, afloat in a cytoplasmic bath,
splitting, re-splitting, until, swollen to fullness,
they stroke through the brimming world.

Milkweed, the scientist, Hans Spemann, thinks,
then peers through a microscope's steady beam
to a shoal of landlocked seeds.
At his back, his newborn stirs in a wicker pram.
And because there is nothing softer at hand

Spemann saws through a two-celled newt egg
with a length of the infant's hair,
the plump globe opening slowly, and the matter inside
already building its new borders.
Two, then. Two lives. And how many sires—

Hans Spemann thinks—and how many heirs?
If only the path were brighter, and the lens
finer. If only the hand were surer
and the blade sharper, and firmer,
and without the glint of time . . .

Desires

In autumn, 1879, on a day like today,
the physicist, Charles Vernon Boys,
touched to a spider's quiet web a silver tuning fork,
its long A swimming a warp line, up and up.
The hour's the same, the hemisphere,
and so the sunlight must have banked at this degree
across his buttoned sleeve, and the steady A
stroked a morning's molecules
much like these—although the note I hear
is organ-cast, cathedral-bound, and the sleeve
this sunlight banks across
drapes in tempera from a saint's clasped hands.

Godless in this god-filled room, I'm drawn less
to the saint's sacrificial fate than to the way
like instruments vibrate sympathetically,
or how this painter's ratio of bone to powdered umber
precisely captures a dove's blunt beak. I'm drawn
to his abidingness, the hands that slowly milked
egg white from its yolk, and ground the madder root,
and shaved the gold, and sealed it all
in a varnish skin (although the skin's a web now,
shot through with cracks).

Perhaps he whistled, low in his teeth,
a tuneless breath that dried the saint's wet eye to matte.
Perhaps he scraped the iris back, and built
the ground, and scraped again, to make the light
interior (then varnished it, to make the light eternal).
Propped on a garden bench, a C-fork buzzed, Boys said,
whenever the A was struck. And the spider whirled.

Then down a warp line, desire's leggy shadow
rushed—and rushed—scraping its beak
on the silver mass, silking the tines,
convinced until the last, Boys said,
all that hummed was food.

Nineteen Thirty-four

Radiant, in the Paris sun, the clustered chairs
and canopies, the clustered leaves, one and one
and one—and down the boulevard, the circus tent
in a blowsy park, the Hospital, boulangeries,
the Institute where Curie turns, then takes
in her blackened, slender fingers a finger-shaped

tube of radiation. And the blue Atlantic, radiant,
the American shore, the gold-flecked palette
Paul Cadmus lifts. It is a midday and sundown
in March. He will paint on the flank of an acrobat
a gilded skin. She will stroke down the test tube
a ticking wand. There is sunlight on their sleeves,

as the equinox shifts and the pale-bricked house
of Physics throws open its smallest doors. Radiant,
the boulevards and shorelines, the peat fields, polders,
steeple tops, the Appalachians, Pyrenees,
the river-etched terraces of Warsaw.
And the circus tent with its acrobats, stern-faced

and gilded, circling the ring on their parallel horses.
Radiant, their sudden shape, like fission's sudden
pyramid: one on the shoulders of two, two
on the shoulders of four, four on the eight
pumping, glistening haunches, and the sixteen
polished hooves, mute in the swirling dust.

Vespers: Gregor Mendel and Steam

Not plumes. Not plumes
from the teapot's throat.
But force, unseen, the space
between plume and throat—pure steam,
a cleft near the porcelain throat.
Nightfall on the teacup, the window,
the breaths of the winter ewes.
Nightfall. Nightfall. Dark breach
between breath and ewe.
And what force, what force, now,
will carry our dormant souls?
Not breath. Not cloud.
Not plume. Not plume. Not
shape—Holy Father—but gap.

Sonnet Crown for Two Voices

The glow, how can I express it? My god,
it lifts from protein flecks, up and across
this crafted lens. From flecks of nothingness,
enlarged twelve hundred times, its simple, cold
fluorescence lifts, green as early pea pods.
Like Mendel's progeny, it blinks across
the vines of probability, the sap-glossed
spindle threads. How Gregor would have swooned.

∎

Again today, soft bandages entwine
my sodden legs: edema's finery.
I know, of course, Death draws his liquid kiss
along my soul, his tepid, sallow brine.
A monk, in love with nature's symmetry,
I complement that kiss. I rise to it.

∎   ∎   ∎

I compliment the kiss. I'd rise to it
in time, my gloved guide says. These clumsy hands
could, in time, trace a cell's meridian
or dip into a nucleus a pipette's
tiny mouth. In time, I'd brush chromatic
residue throughout an egg cell's curved expanse—
but we're just setting slides today, kissing glass
to glass to glass, click by sterile click.

∎

Symmetry. The ram's curled horn. The ermine's tracks.
The leaded windowpanes, mute now with snow.
The hourglass I turn, re-turn (the pressing

down, the rising up). Twin cones. Fused necks.
Its counterpart once toppled us, once blew
across my darkened room a single, flapping wing.

.   .   .

Across our darkened room, it flaps its single wing.
Magnified one hundred times, it skims the scope's
broad screen, dips between the waterweed. Protist,
he says. Not plant, not animal, its wing
a single cell, its cell a self, a kingdom
set apart, both intermediate and whole.
We turn away. Our task's to track the glow
again. A deeper world, fluorescent, green.

.

Midday, October, 1870.
Above, air currents from the west-northwest;
below, air currents from the south: a two-toned
cloud bank sparking. Then from the prelacy
I saw, through sudden hail, a helixed axis
glint. And then the two-coned mass: cyclone.

.   .   .

Out past a two-coned mass it glints, cyclone-
spun or flung by trembling chromatin
quaking through this microworld. Shifting spindles
make the cones; shifting slides — I fear — this windblown
scene. But what veers by, star-shaped, black? And thrown
by what? It's just a speck of retina,
of course. Light's one-celled ash. Vision's glinting
artifact, intermediate and whole.

.

One pressing down, one rising up. And one,
alone, black-robed in the prelacy, convinced
those counterwinds would cancel him, would catch
within their compound eye the black-robed mote
he would become. And still, the scientist
within me watched. I held the desk and watched.

.   .   .

The scientist within me watched the desk
withdraw, and then the scope's glass stage, and then
a pocked, nucleic wall, as down we spun,
the shapes that held the shapes all slipping back,
peripheral. And now, two dye-cast
spindle poles appear, magnetic discs that seem
to summon chromosomes, that seem to bend
the stuff of us: east-southeast, west-northwest.
.

Five seconds long. Its path three fathoms wide.
And through the glass it shot a chink that, until
then, had held the heavens back: an earthen span
of roof tile, flitting like a deadly bird.
Across my desk, it tapped its leaden trill.
Tick. Tick. Tick. Tick. Six inches from my hand.

.   .   .

Tick. Tick. Tick. Tick. Six inches from my hand,
the desk clock turns, but we're outside of time,
our movements inward, vertical, unaligned
with moving on. Within this polar land
a micro-Borealis glows, green-banded
through the protein globes. From jellyfish, my friend

has spliced genes for green fluorescence. They find
expression here, he says. As do we, firsthand.

    ▪

Silence. Infernal symphony of bricks
and wind and breaking glass . . . quieted. At rest
against a wall, the flapping, asymmetric bird
was just a tile. And I, no longer parts—
heart or soul or watching eye—was just
a monk, released to love—again—the world.

                    ▪   ▪   ▪

A monk, released to love the world again—
how Mendel would have blossomed here. Reversed
astronomer, he'd chart these inmost
lights of us: sky-shapes expressed through scrims
of sea. And counting traits, he'd diagram
what shapes await us. As we do now—with dextrous
grace, my gloved friend boasts. (Although, in these frail years,
mere skill seems thin.) Not grace? he asks. Well, mercy, then.

    ▪

Silence, then through the frost of shattered glass
an afterglow arose—or pressed—fully formed
but borderless. As I will be, the swirling world
subtracted from the I of me: wind, chalice,
heartbeat, hand. . . . Weightless, measureless, but beautiful,
the glow. How can I express it, my God?

New Poems

Sketchbook

—Dr. Nicolaas Tulp, 1635

Because, each week, he has entered the body,
its torso, freshly sanitized, its legs and arteries,
the rose curve on the underchin executed so deftly
by the hangman's rope; because he has entered
the forearm and cortex, the lobes and hidden
vortices, deeper, then deeper, until what remains—
shallow, undissected flesh—seems simple lines,
their one dimension shadowless;
and because he is tired and has been himself
a subject,
        Tulp turns his page, then tries again
to sketch a caged orangutan. Placid, insouciant,
the animal slips its shallow glances upward,
downward, from the white-ruffed shape shaping it
to the lap and simple page, as the first lines quicken
and a ratted brow begins. There, a nostril,
and there, a shadowing, a depth that plumps
the cheek pouch, the finger's wrinkled
vortices. Slumped at their separate walls, neither
meets the other's eyes,
        although, equally, each
completes the circling gaze—man to beast to page
to man: two pelt-and-pipesmoke-scented curves,
dimensionless, mammalian. Tick by tick
the minutes pass, page by crumpled page,
Beyond the door, caws and yelps and the clack

of carriage wheels . . . and still they sit,
Tulp, the ape, content to see the shapes
they've known — or felt, or sensed, or turned within —
sloughed in husks across the straw.

Meriwether and the Magpie

Did he know the one as sorrow, the one
he held, gunshot-fallen, its
remarkable long tale . . . beautifully variagated?

For the viewer, fate's in the numbers, legend says:
One magpie for sorrow, two for mirth,
three for a wedding, four for a birth . . .

And wedded in their way they were—Lewis, the bird—
their fragile union finalized *with a narrow ring*
of yellowish black just at the rim of the bird's dim eye.

September. Morning. A breeze
through the aspens, fine. (Five for silver, six for gold . . .)
Two centuries still, until language could cup,

in the binary digits of zero and one, all
it could name. And so he cupped the bird,
and framed in script its glossy frame:

the belly is of a beatifull white . . . the wings . . .
party coloured . . . changeable . . . sonetimes presenting as . . .
orange yellow to different exposures of ligt.

Time still, until sorrow's variegated wing
would bisect the land, would sever from the whole
each singular figure. Here was wonder,

chipped from the western sky, its legs and taloned toes,
black and imbricated, the shifting tint of its shape,
particolored, changeable. (Seven for a secret not to be told.)

...

The wings have nineteen feathers . . . it's usual food
is flesh . . . beautifull . . . yellow . . . a redish indigo blue . . .
at this season single as the halks.

September, the little rhyme fluttering above him,
dragging in from the far Atlantic its swift, domestic echo.
Did he wonder, then, why the story closed so suddenly?

(Eight for heaven, nine for hell, and ten
for the devil's own self.) Why abundance alone
could stop the heart's progression?

Morning. Nine's beak, eight's weightless wings.
Then ten, heartless with promise, sets down
on a dipping branch, the click of its digits—

black and imbricated—beginning
the cycle again: the one and then the nothing
from which the one sets forth.

Dürer near Fifty

At dawn on St. Barbara's Eve, just below
the plateau of his fiftieth year, Albrecht Dürer, first
having purchased spectacles, shoes, and an ivory button,
rode a wheel-etched swath of longitude
from Antwerp toward Zeeland, where a whale—
one hundred fathoms long—pulsed on the dark sand.
First having purchased snuffers and furnace-brown,
and coated the pages of his silverpoint sketchbook,
where his scratch-lines—like pears, or tarnish, or thought—
would gradually ripen, he circled Zeeland's seven shores,
past Goes and Wolfersdyk and *the sunken place*
where rooftops stood up from the water.
Already, from thought, he had sketched a dozen
tail-locked sirens, and once, gossip's composite,
a paisleyed rhinoceros with a dorsal horn—and so
would see firsthand a whale, having changed in Antwerp
a Philips florin, and dined with the Portuguese,
and studied the bones of the giant, Antigoon—
his shoulder blade wider than a strong man's back—
although, in fact, the bones were whale, while the whale
Dürer sailed toward was history, erased by degrees
on the outgoing tide. Still, history tells us,
from his spot on that salty prow, Dürer drew precisely
the unseen sight: the absent arc of its sunken shape,
the absent fluke and down-turned eye,
even, it appears, the absent trench the acid sea
had bitten so seamlessly back into the world.

Navigation

Waves or Moths or whatever it is to be called.

—VIRGINIA WOOLF

If it is to be The Waves, then
the moon, perhaps, weighting a sextant's upper shelf,
with the sea a shelf below some traveler's feet.
Planets, time, position line, position line—
and the place is fixed. Invisibly.

If it is to be The Moths, then
something about their flight. April, perhaps.
In a window, the night-blooming horn
of a gramophone. And over the fields,
moths flying, holding their brief shapes
in constant angle to a planet's light.

If it is to be The Waves—the sextant and salt—
then nothing to see at first but stars
and indices. Not the wake's pale seam.
Not a fin or foremast. Not even
the daylit band of the past,
just under the earth's horizon.

Not yet, at least. No story. (A lamp, perhaps,
a flowerpot.) No past with its child
stopped by a lake in her stiff shoes, toeing
the placid water. Arm's length before her,
in an arc, dollops of bread bob—and beyond
the bread, in a second arc, a dozen,
hand-sized turtles, treading in place.

．．．

They cannot eat, the moths. (A little nectar,
a little sap.) Mandibles gone. Just a slender,
tubal tongue wound like a watch spring
in their hollow throats. And, afraid, the turtles
will not eat, the shadow of the backlit child
rippling toward them as, one by one,
new dollops of bread drop.

If it is to be The Waves, then
cycles on cycles. Eternity. Plurality. (Even the rogue
absorbed.) If it is to be The Moths, then
singleness and brevity. Great brevity—although,
in the leaves behind the child, they are just
beginning to stir, the day's late light

caught in the orbs of the early lamps.
And what is that feeling, shaking its wings
within her? Late day, the leaves and bread
and urgency, all the curious curved shapes
treading in place. If she took a step backward,
would they, in an arc, draw nearer, as a ring
might follow its planet? What then
would she make of the world?

Thoughts Toward
the First Christmas Lecture

—Michael Faraday, 1860

A skin of ice on the inner panes
and Faraday there at the window, his candle flame
burning a peephole. Already morning has warmed
the eaves, the hedgerows thickened by snow.
Children, he thinks, penless, his words underscored
by a tendril of smoke, *I speak to you as a child myself,
amazed by the candle's phenomena: wax and light
and uplifting air, the little cup they form together,
the shallow pool that shivers there.* Over
an empty hummock, parallel tracks of a sleigh soften,
and between the tracks, a horse's widening hoofprints.
Something has scurried across that journey—marten
or hare—bisecting the sleigh tracks. *Consider
that grand circularity, light to fuel to light.
And mystery: a flame that never bites the host
but fattens from it nonetheless.* Perhaps there were
two horses, stepping in tandem down the hummock,
one set of hoofprints absorbing the other. *Children,
we are drawn here to be philosophers, to ask always,
What is the cause? And so you question,
How do flame and fuel meet? And so I say,
By mutual attraction. By the bonding of things
undissolved in each other.* Unlikely, of course, still
were their gaits equal and the reins crossed
their shoulders simultaneously. . . . *Let us turn
to an illustration. Tip your towel to a basin of water,*

194

or better—better!—trouble your mother for a fresh prawn,
then place it tail first in a tumbler, plump head
cupped over the rim. Children, water will climb
through the creature—as fuel climbs a wick!—
by mutual attraction. Already morning
has warmed the eaves, the icicles transparent now,
sloughing their waxy frost—and soon to be prisms,
blinding, as the sun arcs into view. *And what of the flame,*
you ask me, its shadow so solid on the classroom wall?
How can it be both substance and light? Perhaps
there were two horses, stepping in tandem
down the white expanse—soon to be blinding . . .
Children, I must leave you for now with this:
Never is flame of a single body, but a multitude of
successions, so rapid the eye unites them as one.
Something has scurried across the sleigh tracks—
marten or hare—its jittery flight bisecting the hummock,
this way—or that—its slim path both absence and shape,
a low-slung whip of smoke.

Fragments from Venice: Albrecht Dürer

You write for news and Venetian vellum.

I answer: From the sea today a mystery:
proportion's carapaced nightmare: lobster.

You write for burnt glass.

I answer: When tides cross San Marco's cobbles,
bare-shouldered women, bare-shouldered girls,
walk planks to the dark cathedral.

Herr Willibald, my French mantle greets you!
My plumes and misgivings greet you!
Blue-black near the boiling vat, my carapaced neighbor
greets you! (Since dusk, his thin-stalked eyes, like sunflowers,
have tracked my orbiting candle.)

You write that my altarpiece
cups in its wings our destinies.

I answer: In one-point perspective, all lines converge
in a dot of sun far out on the earth's horizon.

I answer: Nightfall makes centaurs of the gondoliers.

I answer: Afloat through the inns, a second perspective
transposes the reign of earth and sun, placing *us*
at the vanishing point.

You write that stubble on the winter fields
supports, through frost, a second field.

...

I answer: When tides withdraw there are birthmarks
on the cobbles. And on the girls' satin slippers
age-rings of silt.

You have seen, secondhand, the centaurs.

I have seen the lobster redden,
then rise like a sun through the boiling water.

Immortality's sign? you ask me. That slow-gaited sea change?
That languorous rising?

I have also seen a comet cross the sky.

Biography

To the dedicated listener, two sounds prevailed that night:
from rafters above the Grand Canal, pigeon snores,
and from the murky water, the tap of gondolas,
like empty walnut shells, against the water steps.
A January Wednesday, 1894, and through those
parenthetic sounds, a figure, Constance Woolson—
novelist, great friend to Henry James—leapt
to her death.
    She fell.
Depressed—*delirious, demented*—she died of—*influenza*—
loving him. *Of unrequited love for James? There is no
evidence.* Seven years before that night, mid-April
through late May, they shared a home in Bellosguardo.
A villa. Voluminous. Then met in Geneva, secretly.
*Secretly? Perhaps, although discretion ruled, not
impropriety.*
    No impropriety? Agreed, although
what ruled was vanity, his need for her devotion.
A spinster, deaf—in just one ear—*and elderly*—a mere
three years his senior—*she was for him primarily a . . .
source—think Alice, Tita, Cornelia, May—
yes, a loyal friend, of course, but . . .*
      Knowing
her death was suicide, James "utterly collapsed."
He could not know, although he suffered, yes. And moved
into her empty rooms, into her empty beds, in Venice, then
in Oxford. *He sought her ghost—as you do now.*
She took herself away—*There is no evidence*—
away from his possession,
      he who so valued possession.

What is biography? What did he mourn? *Analysis?*
Appropriation? She slipped away, as he has slipped
from you. *Anecdote and intuition?* Some weeks beyond
her death, by gondola, James ferried her dresses
to the wide lagoon and, one by one — *Reverence?*
Devotion? —
              lowered them into the water.
They floated back, and back, he said — *Hearsay?*
Secondhand remembrance? — like ghastly, black
balloons, empty and full simultaneously;
although, through salt, silt, and the turning years,
their tidal scrape against the weave —
Reciprocal immortality? — there is no evidence.

From Campalto

We entered Venice by Casa degli Spiriti.

—CONSTANCE FENIMORE WOOLSON

Imagine a white horse, alone in a watery meadow.
Or, alone in a watery meadow, imagine
a white horse. The latter increases your need for me,
your relief in my company, as we walk together
down the story's thin lanes, circling the meadow
and lolling horse, and the gondoliers on the landing
bicker and smoke and shuffle their soft-backed cards.
We have, you as my character and I as your guide,
crossed from Venice on the wide lagoon—
rib-cage deep but for trenches the ships slip through—
and we look toward it now, as one by one
its spires sink through a white fog, that, like your need,
advances.
    To keep me beside you, you speak
of da Vinci's menagerie and the grape skins
best suited for grappa. You would question my friendship
with Henry James—you had hoped, in fact,
for Henry James—but I have grown singular here,
essential to you as our gondoliers, although
they've turned silent, fog-erased, and beacon us closer
by nothing but pipe smoke and their cards' arrhythmic
purr. You would ask of his manner, his temperament,
the nature of our fidelity—two writers enamored
with fiction's grip—of my life in his presence,
of my life in his shadow,
      but are grateful instead

to watch as I pock our trench with pilings
and we feel our way back through the pale lagoon,
column by column, much as the blind
might track the cairns on an ancient path.
You are frightened, I know, in those intervals
when our hands break free and we float
into nothingness. And, yes, I have kept this from you:
increasingly, as the page fills, I am the fabric
of nothingness. You would ask of his voice
and fashion, the nature of our fidelity,
but out from the white fog, here is Casa degli Spiriti,
where up you swing from the swaying boat
and that which remains absorbs me.

Accountancy: Dürer in Antwerp

This many times have I dined with the Factor ///////,
thus often with Stecher /, thus with my Lords //////.
(I am drawn to the fishes. And to citrons—sugared,
like frost over gem stones.)

In trade for my portraits, I have taken
a branch of white coral, a cedarwood rosary, an ounce
of good ultramarine. And a great fish scale
that gauzes the day through its intricate lens.

This many times have mummers amused me ////.

Fourteen stuivers, to date, for raisins. Two for a brush.
One for a buffalo horn. Twenty florins in all
for firewood, flax, one elk's hoof, one parrot cage.
In December, four florins—gold—for a little baboon

who nods like Erasmus when darkness descends.
There is solace, I find, in accountancy,
the prudent, resonant thrift of an evening's meal
preserved in a slant mark, like the solace I feel

with needle and ink, Time's cantering beast
furred for eternity by a burin's bite.

To Johann, one *Passion*. To the surgeon
and house servant, each, a *Life of Our Lady*.
To Konrad, in service of the Emperor's daughter,
one *Melancholy*, three *Marys*, a *Eustace*, a *Nemesis*,
a *Jerome in His Cell*. (Arranged on a wall,
these gifts might mirror our human progression,

as the Great Procession of Our Lady's Assumption—/—
mirrored our ranks, butcher to saint.)

This many times has a fever consumed me /////.
I have dined again // with my Lords.

At the Feast of Our Lady's Assumption, just after
Craftsmen in the Great Procession, but before Prophets
and an armored Saint George, came a crowd of widows
garbed in white linen, accounting for losses amongst us.
Silent, in step, they seemed not shape but vacancy,

alit between mason and seamstress, foot soldier and clerk.
They seemed the space an etch mark frees,
the empty trough that shape awaits.
Grand day, carmine and boot-black and the swirling
world. And those stately widows
defining our borders? These times
did their passing enfold me ///////////////////////////.

Exhibition of a Rhinoceros at Venice

—after the painting by Pietro Longhi, c. 1751

To the tumbler settling on the sawdust street,
with its flames and hoops and carnival swords

swirling up like an alchemist's galaxy, this quiet scene,
glimpsed through a stable's open doors, seems at first

a pond—wall-locked, opaque, lit from above
by the upreaching arc of a white swan.

Then his eyes adjust and the pond is a dampened
stable floor, one ruffle of black rhinoceros. And who

would step forth to restrain him,
if he slipped on his hands and tumbler's knees

in through that black expanse? Or rolled
in a patchwork somersault

like a moon in its blue orbit, while
the swan slowly shifted from beak and wing

to a gaggle of white-masked spectators, mute in the muted
light? Who would object if he nestled beside

that nobility, that count, that willowy, pale contessa
whose throat and white breast

...

first gave to his eyes a swan's neck? From her perch
near a waist-high wall, she is watching

a black-cloaked domino, the dip of his tricornered hat
as he bends to the still rhinoceros,

the wall a border he leans across. And who
would not quicken, as the tumbler does

in his froth of sawdust and shadow, when
the beast slowly raises its earthen mass,

its dusty, furrowed, thick-skinned snout, where
a flag of summer wheat dangles? Just over

its plated hull, just over its rheumy, upturned eyes,
the eyes of the domino hover, dim, plated

in silk, pale as hoops
afloat in some future's flat-lit sky.

Dominance? Challenge? A courtship display?
Who would not wonder what the animal sees

in the white-masked face of such
facelessness, as its toes slowly spread

on the dampened floor, and a shiver of wheat
rises and falls with its breathing?

Details Depicted: Insect and Hair

In the margin between *No reason exists*
and *the innocency of my actings*
in midst of the late revolutions, the writer has circled
a single fly wing, caught years before on the damp page,
now dried to a gauze. Two hundred words
beyond its brittle veins, he falters
and, sensing no stay of his execution, revisits
the world, *the stars over this terraqueous globe*
and *the hazel wheat.* Then he rallies.
A *peculiar magnificence* has filled his cell:
sunset squared through fist-sized windows
and more—there, fast in the page, an arc of amber
beard hair, cupped like calipers toward his drying *m.*
And as he writes *mistaken me for another*
and the scored light fades, he wishes the wing
had followed the hair, as transcendence follows
the life well lived. He wishes the order reversed—
that, first, lit by the hair's prophetic glint,
he might open his story—*Born of worthy parents*—
then weave his history forward, as the paper itself
wove history forward: flax to fabric to shirt
(pockets emptied, buttons snipped) to boiler to pulp
to lifted chin. He knows the power
of augury, of the signs in a perfect path.
He knows, were the wing pinned
near the page's end, he might close
with the grand intangibles, the diaphanous strivings
of citizenship—*allegiance, benevolence,*
the peace and protection of a government—and earn,
by his words, his flight.
                    Late day,

on the wind, two bells ringing in tandem. No help
at all, the artifacts, his useless plea
cresting on the sloughed. What good
to end with the body—*wrought*—
the upward arc reversed? As useless now
to elevate his humanness as to watch
the weightless page withdraw, regain its rags,
its sacking, rope, its bits of salted fishing net.
What good to open with *allegiance* and then
move downward to the flax? What good
to start with *government*, then close
with crows against the sky, or the backward-
swirling, forward-rolling carriage wheels
light on the evening's earth?

Acqua Alta

Vandalism drew us nearer, a slim, graffitied slash
from Icaro to Dedalo across their marble bodies.
In the piazza below our museum window,
carabinieri in sky-blue shirts, and pigeons
and flotsam and teenage boys, drifted together
in the late-day sun—but no,
it wasn't ink-rich aerosol, that looping gash,
just the sculptor's woven cord,
Dedalo to Icaro, lovely in its making. Our spirits
lifted, while over San Marco's quay
the sea quickly rose, glazing the piazza's indentations.
He is tying the wings, someone said, half in pity,
half derision, the myth roped down too literally,
the father too cunning, the son too enraptured.
In from the basin, the sea quickly cast
its daily mass, herringbone brick by brick. A shallow,
dogleg bay, lovely in its making.
He is tying—then the pigeons lifted, and the boys
could not contain themselves
and broke through the glaze in their soft shoes,
churning the water—*the wings*—deafened
by joy and transformation. One, then a dozen,
so suddenly the carabinieri on the dryer reaches
cinched closer together, the moment
half folly, half threat, the Basilica they guarded,
the enamels and marble emperors, the massive,
star-strewn ticking clock, half solid, half,
in reflection, shattered. One, then a dozen,

so suddenly the carabinieri . . . half solid,
half shattered . . . cinched closer, the moment.
He is tying the wings, someone said. In pity. Derision.
It breaks the heart such recklessness.

Salvage

What was the sound, a rasp?
No, not a rasp. *A rattle, then?* No, not that.
And twice it passed over you? I sat
at the waist-gunner window. Night—
and the wingtip's flashing light
bit through slanted snow: green, green.
Then we struck the mountain. *And of eight,*
five were thrown free and survived?
I was cast into deep snow
and plane-shaped debris slipped over me.
Its sound a scraping? No,
not a scraping. It slipped down the canyon wall
and I followed its snow-trough, then
guided the others to me
with blasts from my Mae West whistle.
Yours was a rescue mission, far from war?
I was alone and just overhead in the darkness
snow geese and trumpeter swans passed.
And the green light flashed?
I could hear their bodies working—*And you sat*
at the waist?—ligament, ligature, the labor
of leaving. *In unison, then? A thrum?* No,
each sound in its slender chamber. *And you*
whistled them down to you? Yes.

From the Sea of Tranquillity

Item: After the hopping and gathering,
in that flat, crepuscular light, Armstrong
stroked to the moon's crisp dust, it is said,
Albrecht Dürer's initials, first the A's wide table,
then beneath it, the slumped, dependable D,
the image sinking slowly through that waterless sea,
named less for tides than resemblances.

Item: In the year 1471, in the sixth hour
of Saint Prudentius' Day, Albrecht Dürer was born,
the moon afloat in Gemini's house, and far to the east
Leo rising; an alliance that promised, with travel
and wealth, a slender physique—so slender, in fact,
Dürer slipped from it daily, as, gripped by concentration,
someone else's Albrecht drew a stylus down the grain.

Item: Kicked up through the moon's pale dust, a boot
creates not a scattering but a wave, particles joined
in a singular motion, faithful to the shape
of displacement. Such is the loss of atmosphere,
although aura remains, and time. Think of two men,
each at his milky page, thirst and the dipper
a moment away, and the whole unbroken before them.

—

Flight

Osseous, aqueous, cardiac, hepatic —
back from bone the echoes stroke, back
from the halved heart, the lungs
three years of weightlessness have cinched to gills.
From a leather chaise, the astronaut's withered legs
dangle, as back they come, sounds
a beaked percussion hammer startles into shape.
The physician cocks his head and taps — exactly
as a splitter halves his slate, the metamorphic rock
chisel-shocked, then shocked again, halved

and halved, until a roof appears, black as space.
I'm gaining ground, he says, the astronaut,
who knows, from space, earth is just a blue-green glow,
a pilot light he circled once, lifted, swiftly flown
above the rafters and atmospheres, half himself
and half again some metamorphic click,
extinct as memory. I'm gaining ground,
he says, and back it comes, his glint
of cloud-crossed world: a pilot light
or swaddled leaf, green in the season's infancy.